LOCOMOTION PAPERS

The Helston Branch

by
Stanley C. Jenkins MA

THE OAKWOOD PRESS

© Oakwood Press & S.C. Jenkins 2011

British Library Cataloguing in Publication Data
A Record for this book is available from the British Library
ISBN 978 0 85361 711 2
Second (enlarged) edition 2011, first published 1992

Typeset by Oakwood Graphics.
Repro by PKmediaworks, Cranborne, Dorset.
Printed by Blissetts, Unit 1, Shield Drive, West Cross Industrial Park, TW8 9EX

All rights reserved. No part of this book may be reproduced or transmitted in any form or by any means, electronic or mechanical, including photocopying, recording or by any information storage and retrieval system, without permission from the Publisher in writing.

An Edwardian scene at Helston. Hotel buses mingle with Great Western Buses and charabancs - the vehicle on the right is the Poldhu Hotel bus. *Lens of Sutton Collection*

Front cover: '45XX' class 2-6-2T No. 4505 in the goods yard at Helston on 24th July, 1957. At this time it was the oldest '45XX' class locomotive in service; it was withdrawn in October 1957. *Peter W. Gray*

Rear cover: Reproduction to scale of the one-inch Ordnance Survey map published in 1946 (extract of sheet 189). The entire route of the Helston branch is shown. *Crown Copyright*

Rear cover, inset: The Railway Clearing House map showing the railways west of Penwithers Junction (the junction for the Falmouth branch – just south of Truro). The Great Western Railway bus route from Helston to Lizard Head is shown, as are the bus routes from Penzance to St Just and Sennen respectively. *Oakwood Collection*

Published by The Oakwood Press, 54-48 Mill Square, Catrine, KA5 6RD
01290 551122   www.stenlake.co.uk

Contents

	Introduction	5
	Historical Summary	6
Chapter One	**Origins of the Helston Branch**	
	Pre-railway Helston – Early railway development – The Hayle Railway – Formation of the West Cornwall Railway – Effects of the Railway Mania – Developments in the 1860s – The Helston & Penryn Junction Railway – Formation of the Helston Railway Company – Some details of the Act	7
Chapter Two	**Construction, Opening and Early Years**	
	Cutting the first sod – Preliminaries to construction – Construction begins – Construction resumes - An Agreement with the GWR – The 'Dreaded Navvies' – The Board of Trade Report – Opening of the line – Some details of the line – Early years of the line – The Helston Railway promoters: A further note – The Lizard Light Railway	19
Chapter Three	**The Line in Operation**	
	Operation in the early 20th century – Excursions and tourist traffic – The Lizard Road Motor Servicse – Trains and traffic in the 1930s – Rural collection and delivery services – Other developments - A line of character – World War II	45
Chapter Four	**Through the Window: The Route Described**	
	Gwinear Road – Praze – Nancegollan – Truthall Halt – Helston	75
Chapter Five	**Later History and Minor Details**	
	Dieselization in Cornwall – Road competition – Towards closure – The Beeching period – The withdrawal of passenger services – The post-closure period – Conclusion – Envoi – Trackwork – A note on tickets – Revival at Trevarno	137
Appendix One	**Some Locomotives used on the Helston Branch**	157
Appendix Two	**Chronology of Important Dates**	158
Appendix Three	**Station Facilities**	159
Appendix Four	**Helston in 3mm scale** *by Keith Gowen*	161
	Bibliography	166
	Sources	167
	Index	168

A reproduction of a watercolour painting by Harley Miller entitled *A May Afternoon at Helston Station - 1956*. The train from Gwinear Road has arrived. Shunter Billy Pethick has uncoupled engine No. 4563 which is now running around the carriages. On the spur to the goods shed siding is No. 4570 with driver Bert Rowe chatting to the signalman. To the right of the scene are the coal and builders merchants yards of Gwen & Co. and Harveys and the stores of the flour millers - T.F. Hosking. In the middle of the scene are the sheep and cattle pens and buildings of Sturgess & Co, livestock dealers and slaughterers. Owen Trice was foreman with Cyril Real and Kenneth Edgecumbe managing the beef side of the business and Godfrey Trevains the pigs and sheep. The proximity of the naval air base was, and still is, important to the economy of the area. A group of ratings and WRNS have arrived and a Bedford 'SB' coach from HMS *Seahawk* has been sent down from Culdrose to collect them. Two Western National buses are at the bus stops, these have brought in boxes of flowers from outlying growers. Earlier in the day a train will have brought in consignments of Lyons cakes, to be carried by bus to outlying teashops. Nat Thomas' Humber 'Super Snipe' taxi can be seen as can Helston grammar school pupils. Nelson Cleave, the postman, has arrived with his mail van and PC Perry is keeping an eye on the scene with station master Arthur Strong. Working in the garden of 'Bodrean' is Mr Pearce, the inventor of the rod lubricator, a system readily adopted by locomotive builders everywhere. Miss Foy Quiller-Couch is a familiar local character with her pony and trap, she is talking with Tommy Champion who has a trolley full of boxes of cream from Trenear and Treloquithack dairies. Henry Collins is known locally as the 'Rabbit Man'. His shed opposite the station was the receiving point for dead rabbits brought in by local farmers, and which he would hang up under the eaves. When he was not there himself to deal with the farmers, the station porters would stand in for him. Quantities of rabbits were sent daily from Helston to Liverpool and Birmingham. Henry Collins was also an agent for a number of local growers. T.H. Collins & Son sent potatoes and broccoli weekly from the station, as well as dozens of boxes of anemones which Henry grew at Gweek.

Helston Folk Museum

Introduction

The Helston branch was the southernmost railway on the British mainland, and also the very last branch line to have been built in south-western Cornwall. Sadly, it was also one of the first to close, and perhaps for this reason it has not enjoyed the attention that has been lavished upon certain neighbouring ex-Great Western Railway (GWR) lines. Fortunately, the branch from Gwinear Road to Helston had at least one champion in the person of G.A. Anthony, whose book *The Hayle, West Cornwall & Helston Railways* (Oakwood Library No. 21) did much to keep the memory of the line alive. Mr Anthony (a former station master at Plymouth North Road) was well-qualified to write about the branch, having once served as a clerk at Helston.

The original version of *The Hayle, West Cornwall & Helston Railways* was out of print for several years, but in 1990 the present author was asked to revise and expand Mr Anthony's book. It was initially felt that the text should be retained in a more or less unaltered form, but at that point certain problems arose; in particular, the original text of *The Hayle, West Cornwall & Helston Railways* which was - as its name implied - a combined history of three distinct railways in West Cornwall. The narrative also seemed slightly unbalanced, in that it devoted much space to the Helston branch while largely ignoring the nearby St Ives line. Moreover, the Helston branch route was described in some detail, whereas the route of the West Cornwall main line was ignored.

For these reasons the publishers suggested that *The Hayle, West Cornwall & Helston Railways* might be re-issued as *The West Cornwall Railway* (Oakwood Library No. 122), leaving the field clear for me to begin work on a new Helston monograph, which was first published in 1992.

This new, much-expanded edition of *The Helston Branch* adopts a broadly chronological framework, in that Chapter One deals with the pre-history of the line, while Chapters Two and Three deal with the construction, history and operation of the railway from its incorporation until the end of the GWR era. Chapter Four is a detailed examination of the stations and route of the line, while Chapter Five is devoted to the British Railways period. A considerable amount of additional material has been added, including details of the present-day 'Helston Railway', which has been re-established as a 'heritage line' and an added attraction at Trevarno Gardens, between Nancegollan and Truthall Halt.

Thanks are due to all who have helped in the preparation of this volume, and its 1992 predecessor, particularly the staffs of the University of Leicester Library and the Science Museum Library, London; also Lens of Sutton, Chris Turner, the late John M. Strange and Martin Matthews of the Helston Folk Museum.

Stanley C. Jenkins
Witney
Oxfordshire
2011

Historical Summary

Company of origin

Helston Railway, formed by Act of Parliament dated 9th July, 1880 to build a railway from Gwinear Road to Helston. The authorized capital was £70,000 in £20 shares, and £23,333 by loan. The completed line was worked by the Great Western Railway, and the Helston Railway Company was absorbed by the GWR by Act of 2nd August, 1898.

Length of line

Built to standard gauge (4 ft 8½ in.) for a distance of 8 miles 67 chains (Gwinear Road to Helston passenger station), and 8 miles 76 chains (Gwinear Road to terminal buffer stops at Helston).

Date of opening

Monday 9th May, 1887 (public and ceremonial opening).

Mode of operation

The single line between Gwinear Road and Helston was initially worked by train staff without block telegraph. Later, the line was worked by electric train staff, with an intermediate crossing loop near Nancegollan station. In 1937, the latter station was remodelled to allow passing to take place within the confines of the station - up and down platforms being provided for the first time.

Typical motive power

Small GWR 0-4-2Ts and 0-4-4Ts worked the line for many years, together with 0-6-0 saddle tanks. In later Great Western days the route was usually worked by '45XX' class 2-6-2Ts of the 4500-4575 (small tank) series. Class '22' diesel-hydraulics appeared around 1961, and a member of this class worked the last passenger train in 1962.

Date of closure

The Helston branch was closed to passenger traffic with effect from Monday 5th November 1962, with the last trains running on Saturday 3rd November, 1962. The route remained open for freight traffic for a further two years until October 1964.

Chapter One

Origins of the Helston Branch

The Helston branch line, opened in 1887, was the last section of railway to be built in West Cornwall, and it may well be wondered why it was that such a go-ahead town as Helston, with its long history as a tin mining centre, and traditions of public service, did not have a railway long before then. The 8 mile 67 chain railway that eventually linked Helston to the main line at Gwinear Road brought great prosperity, met the needs of an expanding local economy, and laid the foundations of the tourist industry upon which so many people now depend for a living. However, the story of Helston and its railway does not begin with the efforts which resulted in the opening of the branch line in May 1887; it started much earlier, and it would therefore be useful to say a few words about Helston in pre-railway days.

Pre-railway Helston

Helston, which probably derived its name from 'Henlis' - the old court - has a long history, stretching back to Celtic times. The Domesday survey of 1086 records that 'Henlistone' had formerly belonged to King Harold, while Daniel Defoe described it as 'large and populous, with four spacious streets, a handsome church, and a good trade'.

A tin mining centre and market town from the earliest times, Helston was one of the places named as a 'coinage' town in Edward I's Charter to the Tinners in 1305 - though tin was not actually coined there until the 16th century. Blocks of smelted tin would be brought into the town from the surrounding mining districts to be assayed and tested for purity before receiving the stamp of the Duchy of Cornwall. It is interesting to note that the former Chapel of Our Lady was adapted for use as a 'Coinage Hall' at the time of the Reformation - the street in which it stood eventually becoming known as Coinagehall Street.

The tin mining industry was at its peak during the late 18th and early 19th centuries, by which time around 100 mines were said to be working in the Wendron, Sithney, Breage and Godolphin areas. There were numerous mines along the Cober Valley to the north of Helston, while the famous Wheal Vor mine near Godolphin was probably the richest mine in all Cornwall (if not the world).

Many hundreds of miners worked in the area, and on Saturdays the roads from Sithney, Breage and Wendron would be crowded with people on their way to Helston to spend their wages. Many miners frequented the beer shops or 'kiddlywinks' in the town, and fights often took place; it is estimated that, in the early 19th century, the town was enjoying upwards of £10,000 worth of trade a week as a result of its proximity to the mining districts.

Helston was, by the mid-19th century, an important local centre, with a population of about 3,500. A contemporary account described the town as follows:

It is regularly and neatly built, and comprises four large streets in cruciform arrangement with a handsome and spacious market house and town hall at the centre, a police station, church, four dissenting chapels, a literary institution and reading room, a dispensary and a workhouse. The town is a seat of petty sessions and a polling place; was made a borough by King John; sent two members to Parliament from the time of Elizabeth I till the Reform Act but now sends one member; is governed by a mayor, four aldermen and twelve councillors; has a head post office, three banking offices, one or two good inns and a grammar school. Markets are held on Wednesdays and Saturdays and fairs several times a year, and there is considerable trade done with neighbouring mines.

The 'four large streets' referred to in this extract were Coinagehall Street and Wendron Street which, together, formed the long axis of Helston's cruciform layout. These two streets were intersected by Meneage Street and Church Street to form a roughly cross-shaped arrangement, while other streets and alley-ways branched out from the four main thoroughfares.

In earlier days the River Cober, which flowed past the town near lower end of Coinagehall Street, was navigable for all or part of the year, and this waterway formed a useful means of transport for the town. Unfortunately Helston's rôle as a port was curtailed by the formation of the 'Loe Bar' at the mouth of the Cober, which blocked the river and thereby turned its lower reaches into a large lake known as the Loe Pool. Thereafter, tin was exported from Helston via the nearby Helford River, and Gweek - as the tidal limit of that river - became Helston's principal port.

In 1796, it was suggested that a navigable waterway might be dug across the Cornish peninsula between the Hayle River at St Erth and the Helford River near Gweek, thereby creating a useful link between the north and south coasts of Cornwall. The proposed 'Helston Canal' would have been about 14 miles long, with inclined planes at St Erth, Bosence, Drym, Nancegollan, Trannack, Mellangoose and Gweek. A route was surveyed by Robert Fulton (1765-1815), the American engineer, who estimated that the 'Helston Canal' would cost £32,000. The large number of inclined planes that would have been required underlines the fact that Cornish topography was not really suitable for ambitious canal schemes, and it perhaps comes as no surprise that the Hayle to Helford canal scheme was never implemented.

Early railway development

The conditions needed for pioneering railway developments were present in abundance in early 19th century Cornwall. The local tin and copper mines were at their peak in terms of production and investment, and the mines were already served by short lengths of primitive tram lines. As the Industrial Revolution gathered momentum, the Cornish mines acquired large numbers of steam pumping engines, which were needed to prevent the workings from flooding. This, in turn, encouraged the growth of engineering skills, and in this context West Country engineers and inventors played an important role in the development of new technologies. The first practical steam pumping engine, for example, was invented by Thomas Newcomen (1663-1729) of Dartmouth, while the world's very first locomotives were developed in Cornwall; in 1784, William Murdock constructed and tested a working model at Redruth, while in 1796 Richard Trevithick (1771-1833) built a full-size engine. Trevithick's locomotive made its first successful run at Camborne in 1801, but as the roads of the period were so bad, he decided to run his engine on rails, and in this way the world's first railway locomotive was created.

Perhaps inevitably, Cornish landowners, mine owners and entrepreneurs became prolific railway promoters, and some of the earliest lines in the country were built in Cornwall. On 25th October, 1809, construction of Cornwall's first railway was started at Portreath, when the prominent mine owner Lord de Dunstanville laid the first rail of the Poldice Tramroad. This pioneering line was built as a transport link between the mines around Scorrier and the harbour at Portreath - which had itself been constructed in the 18th century as an outlet for local copper ore. The first section of the Poldice line was probably in use by 1810, and the horse-worked tramway was in full operation by 1812.

In 1819, a Prospectus was issued for construction of a similar tramway from Hayle to Helston, while in the early 1820s the pioneer railway promoter William James (1771-1837) surveyed a number of possible lines in the Cornish mining areas. In 1825, plans were drawn up for a tram line between Penryn and Redruth, with a branch to Wendron and thence to Helston. In the event, these schemes were abortive, but they served to focus attention on the concept of improved transport links between the mining districts and convenient ports such as Hayle and Portreath.

Capital for further investment was, at this time, readily available, and Cornwall was replete with capable engineers and surveyors with the ability to plan and construct longer, more ambitious lines such as the Redruth & Chacewater Railway, which was sanctioned by Parliament on 17th June, 1825, with powers for the construction of a mineral line from the Gwennap mines near Scorrier to Narobo Quays, on Restronguet Creek. This 4 ft gauge line was officially opened on 30th January, 1826, when some of the promoters rode by gravity from Wheal Buller Mine to Devoran, the return journey being made behind a horse. Traffic soon reached 60,000 tons per annum, and by the 1830s the Redruth & Chacewater Railway was making profits of £3,000 a year.

The Hayle Railway

The obvious success of the Redruth & Chacewater Railway led to the promotion of further lines, the most important of these being the Hayle Railway, which was incorporated by Act of Parliament on 27th June, 1834, with powers for the construction of a railway from Hayle, in the parish of St Erth, to Tresavean Mine, in the parish of Gwennap. As first authorized, the Hayle Railway would have included branch lines to Helston, Tresavean, Roskear, Wheal Crofty and the Sandhills at Hayle, but on 4th July, 1836 the company obtained a new Act, permitting deviations of the original route, and a branch from Pool to Portreath in place of the suggested line to Helston.

The railway builders made very good progress, and the Hayle Railway main line was substantially complete between Hayle and Pool by 1837. Good progress had also been made on the branch to Portreath, and it was therefore decided that the line would be brought into operation between Hayle, Pool and Portreath, before the main line was completed throughout to its eastern terminus at Redruth. The railway was opened from Hayle to 'Pool' (Carn Brea), and on to Portreath, on Saturday 23rd December, 1837. The opening was celebrated in comparatively modest style by a locomotive bringing a train of coal wagons from Hayle to Pool, and then proceeding along the branch line to Portreath in order to collect another train.

Work was, meanwhile, proceeding apace on the remaining part of the main line between Portreath Junction and Redruth, and this section was officially opened on Thursday, 31st May, 1838, on which day the Hayle Railway main line was completed throughout between Hayle and Redruth. It had initially been anticipated that the public opening would take place on 4th June, 1838, but as this was Whit Monday the Directors decided that there would be so many high-spirited spectators that 'accidents might occur' and the opening was therefore postponed until 11th June. The branch from Redruth Junction to Tresavean was opened just 12 days later, and thus, by the middle of 1838, the 17¼ mile Hayle Railway system was completed.

The Hayle line was constructed to the national gauge of 4 ft 8½ in., and it was worked by a mixture of locomotives and rope-worked inclines. Passengers were carried on a regular basis from Monday 22nd May, 1843, the inauguration of passenger services being celebrated in appropriate style, 'amid much public rejoicing, in which the bands of the neighbourhood took part'. The first timetable provided three trains each way between Hayle and Redruth.

Formation of the West Cornwall Railway

In 1845 the promoters of an undertaking known as the West Cornwall Railway (WCR) presented a Bill to Parliament seeking consent for the construction of railways from Truro to Redruth, and from Hayle to Penzance, in connection with the existing Hayle Railway. The original scheme envisaged that the West Cornwall line would be an upgraded version of the Hayle Railway. Although the sections from Truro to Redruth and from Hayle to Penzance would be entirely new construction, trains would continue to use the Hayle Railway between Redruth and Hayle. In the event, these proposals were rejected by Parliament on the grounds that the steeply-graded Hayle Railway was unsuitable for use as a through route for main line passenger traffic.

Undeterred by the failure of their 1845 Bill, the West Cornwall Railway promoters prepared a revised scheme for submission in the 1846 session. As in 1845, the proposals included new lines from Truro to Redruth and from Hayle to Penzance, but at the same time it was suggested that the Hayle line would be substantially rebuilt, with extensive deviations to obviate the worst inclines en route. The 1846 West Cornwall Bill was, moreover, backed by the Great Western Railway, and with Isambard Kingdom Brunel as its Engineer the scheme seemed destined for success. Parliament was of the same opinion, and on 3rd August, 1846 the West Cornwall Railway Bill received the Royal Assent.

The resulting Act of Parliament (9 & 10 Vict. cap. 336) provided consent for the construction of a broad gauge railway commencing 'in the Parish of Kenwyn in the County of Cornwall' to 'the East Cliff at Penzance', with branches to Truro River and other specified places. To pay for their scheme the West Cornwall Railway supporters were authorized to raise the sum of £500,000 in £20 shares, with borrowing powers for a further £165,000. The gauge of the 25 mile railway was to be the same as 'that of the Great Western Railway', subject to the liability to lay additional rails of 'the gauge of any railway' which might later be constructed through Cornwall.

The first ordinary meeting of the newly-constituted West Cornwall Railway Company was held on 22nd December, 1846, and at that meeting it was agreed that authority should be given to the WCR Directors to apply to Parliament in the ensuing session for powers for the construction of 'a branch railway to St Ives, with a short branch or extension therefrom to Norwaymens' Wharf in the Parish of Lelant, and also to construct and enlarge certain wharfs or quays at or near Hayle, all in the County of Cornwall'.

Effects of the Railway Mania

There were, by the mid-1840s, several other proposals for railways in the west Cornwall area. Indeed, such schemes were now coming thick and fast, for the 1840s were the period of the 'Railway Mania', in which new companies were floated recklessly with little or no regard for national, or even local planning. In 1846, for instance, plans were deposited for a line from Helston to Penryn, via Gwealmayo, Tregarrick, Gweek, Merther, Constantine, Holland Mill and Mabe. The necessary financial support was not forthcoming and, sadly, the proposals fell through. Of this scheme G.J.C. Cunnack of Helston wrote:

> During the excitement of 1845, a line, or rather a company, was attempted for the making of a railway from Helston to Penryn, got up by some local attorneys and others. Several Helston businessmen allowed themselves to be nominated provisional committeemen, and found to their cost (the scheme having found no financial support) that they were saddled with the expense arising from the surveying and Parliamentary applications. The line, perhaps fortunately for Helston, left its remembrance as 'The Tatey Line.

Unfortunately a series of abysmally-wet summers and failed harvests during the later 1840s led to a major economic crisis. In these unhappy conditions it became increasingly difficult for companies such as the West Cornwall Railway to raise their authorized capital, and in these circumstances the promoters were unable to begin work on their schemes. The West Cornwall company had, however, taken possession of the Hayle Railway in November 1846, and for the next few years the West Cornwall Railway continued to provide passenger and freight services over the existing line, using the Hayle Railway's locomotives and rolling stock.

Eventually, a gradual improvement in the economy enabled the WCR promoters to implement their scheme, and in 1850 the West Cornwall Railway company obtained new powers, permitting deviations of the Hayle line and allowing the company to construct the Truro and Penzance extensions as standard-gauge lines. In this modified form a line through to Penzance was opened on 11th March, 1852, while on 25th August, 1852 the eastern extension was completed from Redruth to a terminus at Higher Town, near Penwithers, on the western outskirts of Truro.

There had, in the interim, been an important development, in that an entirely separate company known as the Cornwall Railway had been incorporated by Act of Parliament on 3rd August, 1846 (9 & 10 Vict. cap. 335) with powers for the construction of a railway between Plymouth, Truro and Falmouth. The Cornwall Railway was, by any definition, a major concern with an authorized capital of no less than £1,600,000 in £20 shares; this was, needless to say a phenomenal sum by early Victorian standards, and it underlines the fact that the projected railway was conceived as an important broad-gauge main line that would form the primary means of long-distance communication between Cornwall and the distant Metropolis.

After many vicissitudes, the Cornwall Railway was opened between Plymouth and Truro, a distance of 45 miles, on 4th May, 1859, and this heavily-engineered route was completed throughout to its western terminus at Falmouth on 24th August, 1863. This established railway communication between London and west Cornwall.

The appearance of the Cornwall Railway had obvious ramifications in terms of the hitherto localized West Cornwall company, and on 15th August, 1853 the WCR obtained Parliamentary consent for two new lines in the Truro area. One of these lines, known as the 'Extension Railway', ran from the original West Cornwall terminus at Higher Town to wharves on the Truro River at Newham. The other new line, described as the 'Junction Railway', ran from Higher Town to the Cornwall Railway's Truro station. The Extension line was opened on 16th April, 1855, while the Junction line was opened on 1st August, 1859, thereby placing the standard-gauge West Cornwall Railway in contact with the broad-gauge Cornwall line.

In later years, the Cornwall Railway and the West Cornwall route would both be incorporated into a unified Great Western main line between London and Penzance, but this was by no means apparent in the late 1850s and early 1860s - when various grandiose schemes were being suggested for whole systems of lines in the Cornish peninsula.

The Helston & Penryn Junction Railway

There was, as yet, no rail link to Helston or the Lizard, but local traders and residents continued to hope that a line would one day be built. Their expectations were raised during the 1860s, when proposals were put forward for an ambitious scheme which, if successful, would have covered much of south-western Cornwall. This scheme, known as 'The Cornwall Union Railway', envisaged the construction of the following lines:

1. Helston to Penryn via Gweek and Constantine (as in 1846).
2. Helston to Penzance, starting at Tresprison then via Gwealfolds, Lowertown, Town Mills, Newham, Sithney, Wheal Vor, Godolphin, Retallack, Halamanning, thence north to Marazion, crossing the West Cornwall line, and on to Penzance.
3. A branch from Halamanning to a point between St Erth and Lelant.
4. A line from Penzance to St Just, through Trencere, Heymoor, Poltaggan Mill, Trevean, Penhale, Bojuthno, Boscoswell, Trewelland, Botallack, and Kenidjack to St Just.

The Helston to Penzance, Penzance to St Just and St Erth to Halamanning proposals wore dropped on account of engineering difficulties, high cost, and the uncertain prospects of local mining (which were becoming apparent at that time). The Helston to Penryn scheme was, however, taken up by a group of local landowners, bankers and solicitors, the necessary Parliamentary Bill being sponsored by John St Aubyn, John Jope Rogers, S.Morley Grylls, John Kendall and Alfred Jenkin.

On 14th July, 1864 the Helston & Penryn Junction Railway (H&PJR) received the Royal Assent (27 & 28 Vict. cap. 197), and the promoters were thereby empowered to raise £120,000 in £20 shares, and £40,000 by loans, to build a nine mile, broad gauge branch, which would commence in the parish and borough of Helston and terminate by a junction with the Falmouth branch of the Cornwall Railway in the Borough of Penryn and Parish of St Gluvias. John St Aubyn MP, John Jope Rogers, John Kendall, J.F. Basset and Major Grylls became the first H&PJR Directors, joined by Thomas Agar Robartes MP, of Llanhydrock - the Member of Parliament for East Cornwall and an important local mine owner with substantial interests in the Redruth area.

The first meeting of the newly-constituted Helston & Penryn Junction Railway Company was held at Truro in October 1864, and in an atmosphere of growing enthusiasm the scheme's supporters were told that their Act had been obtained 'without contest', and a line to Helston would soon be made. The suggested route avoided heavy earthworks, and the line authorized by the Act 'for making a railway from Helston to Penryn in the county of Cornwall' could be 'very economically constructed'. It was envisaged that the new branch would pass through the parishes of Wendron, Constantine, Mabe, Budock and St Gluvias to converge with the Falmouth branch at a point 'one chain or thereabouts south of the west platform of Penryn station'; heavy cuttings would not be needed, and the completed line would thus be much more lucrative than the heavily-engineered Cornwall Railway.

In optimistic vein, the ambitious promoters of the Helston & Penryn Junction Railway claimed that their line would 'yield a fair percentage', while the finished railway would tap a district which produced 'the finest granite in the Kingdom'. Lucrative stone traffic would (it was hinted) be highly profitable, but in addition to this guaranteed source of bulk freight traffic, the hoped-for branch would pass through an agricultural district 'capable of producing large quantities of early vegetables for the London markets', and this would contribute to the healthy profits that were expected to accrue to the proprietors of the railway.

Unfortunately, the investing public was wary of these claims, and by 1866 (when the failure of bankers Overend & Gurney plunged the financial world into depression) the Helston & Penryn Junction scheme had been abandoned. The opening of the Cornwall Railway's branch from Truro to Falmouth in August 1863 had, nevertheless, been a source of encouragement for those hoping to bring railway communication to Helston and the Lizard peninsula, and although many local people had lost money in the Helston & Penryn Junction venture, there were persistent attempts to secure the desired rail link.

A line from Helston to the Falmouth branch at Penryn continued to be strongly favoured locally and in 1872 plans were again deposited, this time for a line to be known as the 'Penryn & Helston Railways and Tramways', from Helston to Wendron, thence to Sevorgan, Retallack, Holland Mills, Mabe and Penryn, with a tramway extension to Budock. Although these proposals were fully approved by the Cornwall Railway, the Bill was withdrawn suddenly in 1874 and the promoters were again the losers.

By this time, the mining of tin and copper had seriously declined. Many mines had been completely worked out, and much of the remaining ore was being obtained from deeper and deeper workings, thus increasing the cost of production, reducing the margin of profit and, in many cases, causing the adventurers to suffer severe losses. It is not surprising, therefore, that as far as Helston was concerned, there was less enthusiasm for any new railway venture. Seven years went by before there was fresh thinking which brought renewed determination to get a railway to Helston.

Formation of the Helston Railway Company

In 1879, the Helston Railway Company was formed with a provisional capital of £70,000 in 3,500 twenty pound shares, to construct a railway from Gwinear Road station, on the West Cornwall Railway to Helston - the long-cherished idea of a branch from Penryn having, at long last, been abandoned. The scheme was fully supported by the land-owning community, its principal supporters being W. Molesworth St Aubyn, William Bickford-Smith, Mr T.S. Bolitho, Mr J.R. Daniell and other local gentlemen.

The Helston Railway was, in many ways, the lineal descendant of the Helston & Penryn Junction Railway and the other abortive schemes but, perhaps significantly, this new proposal was a more modest affair than many of its ill-fated predecessors. The proposed line would be no more than eight or nine miles in length and, with a solid body of local support, it appeared that the Helston Railway Company stood every chance of success.

The scheme is said to have evolved following a casual conversation between Mr Daniell, a solicitor from Camborne, and William Bickford-Smith, who said that 'it was a wonder that a line from Gwinear Road had never been thought about'. The matter was brought to the attention of T.S. Bolitho, who 'warmly approved of it' and considered the project to be eminently practicable. A provisional committee was formed, and Sylvanus W. Jenkin (1821-1911), of Liskeard, was engaged to survey the route. He suggested that the proposed line from Gwinear Road was 'the best that could be found', and estimated that it could be built at a cost of less than £80,000, or £9,500 per mile. It was felt that the Gwinear Road route had three distinct advantages over the alternative route from Penryn - it would be shorter, cheaper to build, and the completed line would, moreover, open-up a district in the western part of Cornwall that had not, hitherto, enjoyed the benefits of a rail link to the outside world.

Having decided to proceed with their scheme, the leading supporters held a public meeting in the Guildhall at Helston on 5th November, 1879, 'for the purpose of considering the steps to be taken in order to secure the construction of a railway'. Opening the meeting, Mr Daniell explained that the route from Gwinear Road had already been surveyed and he asked Mr Jenkin to say a few words about the proposed line:

> The scheme provided for a narrow (i.e. 4 ft 8½ in. gauge) railway from Gwinear Road. The distance was only about 8½ miles, about 2½ miles less than the route from Penryn. Most of the line was over very level ground, and the only obstacle was a valley near Helston, which would have to be crossed by a viaduct. The advantage of a having a narrow gauge line to join the West Cornwall line was that they could make better terms with the Great Western. It was necessary to make terms with that company if any line was ever to be constructed so far west as Helston. He was not prepared to say what negotiations had taken place between the persons who were promoting the line and the Great Western Company; he would only say that the negotiations were far advanced and in a very satisfactory condition, and there was a great wish on the part of the Great Western Company that the line should be constructed. The promoters hoped that ultimately a satisfactory arrangement would be made with the Great Western Company to work the line.

Mr Jenkin emphasised that the railway from Gwinear Road to Helston was 'by far the cheapest line that could be made', and he added that he knew of a contractor who would be prepared to undertake the work of construction within the estimated cost of £80,000, taking shares in the company in part-payment. When the resulting applause had subsided, a member of the public asked if provision could be made for a branch to Porthleven? Mr Jenkin replied that this had not been lost sight of, 'but the matter was one which would have to be considered subsequently, and not immediately in connection with the question of constructing a line'.

At the end of the proceedings it was agreed that 'the meeting was of the opinion that the scheme proposed would meet the requirements of the district', and that a 'local committee' would be formed to confer with the promoters, while William Bickford-Smith and other leading supporters would negotiate with the Great Western Railway about terms for working the proposed Helston line.

In its Prospectus, the company claimed that the shortest and cheapest route had been selected, as well as the one most 'likely to secure the greatest traffic'. The proposed terminus at Helston was chosen with a view to extension at a later date to the Lizard or other adjacent districts. The tourist trade had increased considerably since the opening of the Cornwall Railway to Falmouth in 1863; this had introduced the lovely villages in the Lizard peninsula and the Meneage district to a growing clientele and it was confidently anticipated that a railway to Helston would improve communications still further, and so increase holiday traffic from London and the Midlands with passengers travelling by rail to Helston instead of via Falmouth.

An early view of Coinagehall Street, looking west, with the Angel Hotel to the left.
Oakwood Collection

A postcard view of the Lizard, looking south-westwards from Housel Bay towards Bumble Rock, with the Lizard Lighthouse visible to the right. *Author's Collection*

ORIGINS OF THE HELSTON BRANCH

The company had evidently conducted a considerable amount of 'market research' and the Prospectus stated that:

> Helston is the centre of an important and productive agricultural district; a large passenger, goods, mineral and fish traffic may be expected, while a railway will give the greatest impetus to the development of market gardening, for which the district is so admirably adapted. The traffic between Helston and the towns and districts of Penzance, Marazion, Hayle, St Ives, Camborne and Redruth is already large, and will doubtless increase with improved facilities for transport.

It was calculated that, based upon the number of persons entering and leaving Helston daily, and of the tonnage of goods traffic of the borough and district, coupled with the experience of existing lines, an average revenue of at least £20 per mile could be expected.

The Great Western Railway Company was in favour of the line being constructed, and an agreement was entered into with them that their shareholders would be recommended to work the branch when completed, at 50 per cent of the gross receipts. These terms were considered to be favourable, and it was believed they would leave a good profit on the small amount of capital required.

The total length of the proposed railway was about eight miles, and it was believed that, after paying 50 per cent of the receipts to the Great Western Railway, the weekly average traffic returns of £20 per mile, 'would leave about £4,500 a year, an ample revenue to admit of a liberal interest or dividend on invested capital, after making allowance for the small necessary standing charges'. Moreover, the promoters hoped that, as the district developed, an even greater traffic return would result. In support of this claim they pointed out that although the published traffic returns had been 'very carefully taken', the estimated receipts did not include additional traffic from Penryn, Truro or Falmouth - some of which was expected to flow over the Helston line once the new branch was in operation.

The Engineer estimated that construction costs for the whole line, including the cost of land and all contingencies, would not exceed £70,000 and, as intimated at the Guildhall meeting, a 'responsible contractor' had offered to complete the work for this figure, taking a 'considerable number' of shares in part payment for building the line.

In November 1879 the promoters gave formal notice that they intended to make an application to Parliament in the ensuing session for an Act to incorporate a company with powers to make and maintain a railway from Gwinear Road to Helston, with 'all necessary and proper stations, works, and conveniences connected therewith'. The proposed Helston branch was described as a railway:

> Situate wholly in the County of Cornwall, commencing by a junction with the West Cornwall Railway of the Great Western Railway Company, in the Parish of Gwinear, on a siding of the said West Cornwall Railway, at or near the Gwinear Road Station, at a point 44 yards or thereabouts, measured in an easterly direction from the point where the said siding leaves the down line, and on the south side thereof, passing thence from,

through, or into the several parishes or places of Gwinear, Crowan, Sithney, Wendron and Helston, and terminating in the borough and ecclesiastical parish of Helston, in a field belonging to Adolphus William Young, Esq., MP., and occupied by Thomas Oliver, lying on the west side of the turnpike road or public highway leading from Helston to Redruth, numbered 277 on the tithe apportionment map of the ecclesiastical parish of Helston, at or near a point in the said field 44 yards or thereabouts from the north-east corner thereof.

The Helston Railway Bill was sent up to Parliament in time for the 1880 session, and on 10th February, 1880 *The Journal of the House of Commons* reported that the Bill for 'Construction of a railway from the Gwinear Road station of the West Cornwall Railway Company to Helston' had successfully passed its first and second readings.

It seemed that the Helston Railway Bill would have an easy passage through both houses, but unfortunately Parliament was dissolved before the scheme could receive the Royal Assent. This was not in the event a major problem, and on 21st May, 1880 a new Parliament gave the Helston Railway Bill a nominal 'first and second reading'. The Bill was read for a third time on 1st June, and having been approved by the Lords, it received the Royal Assent on 9th July, 1880.

Some details of the Act

The Helston Railway Act provided Parliamentary consent for the construction of a branch railway commencing, as described in the Bill, by a junction with the West Cornwall line of the Great Western Railway 'on a siding near the Gwinear Road Station thereof', and terminating in the borough and ecclesiastical parish of Helston 'in a field on the west side of the turnpike road or public highway leading from Helston to Redruth'. The authorized line would be 8 miles 67 chains in length, and to pay for its construction the promoters were empowered to raise £70,000 in ten pound shares, with borrowing powers of up to £23,333.

Five years were allowed for completion of the works, and the proposed tolls for first, second and third class passengers were 2*d*., 1½*d*., and 1*d*. per mile respectively. General merchandise would be carried at the rate of 1*d*. per ton per mile, 1½*d*. per ton per mile, 2*d*. per ton per mile or 3*d*. per ton per mile, according to a scale of specified charges.

In July 1881 the provisional Directors held a further meeting in the Guildhall at Helston, and they were able to announce that 'a capitalist' had been found who was willing to undertake the construction of the line and hand it over to the company in full working order. When the assembled shareholders had unanimously agreed to this proposal, the next item of business was the election of Directors, and William Bickford-Smith, Daniel Wise Bain, William Bolitho Junior, Richard Skews Martyn and Richard G. Rows were duly elected as the first Directors of the Helston Railway Company. It seemed that, after years of prevarication and delay, the hoped-for branch line was about to be built, and as the summer of 1880 turned to autumn, the people of Helston were confident that their railway would soon become a reality.

Chapter Two

Construction, Opening and Early Years

Having obtained their Act of Incorporation, the supporters of the Helston Railway were eager to begin work on the 8¾ mile line, but the next few months were, of necessity, devoted to preliminary matters such as the raising of capital. In this context, it is refreshing to record that, despite the abysmal failure of all previous attempts to bring rail communication to Helston, the townspeople were still highly enthusiastic, and they gave their full support to the project. According to a contemporary report, 'When the scheme was brought before the public there was great enthusiasm, and the townspeople came forward and took up twenty pound shares in a way that surprised themselves, and others more so'.

Cutting the first sod

The main contract for construction of the branch was awarded to Messrs Maddison & Co., Mr Maddison having agreed to 'complete the line and have it ready for traffic within two years'. The contract provided for the construction of a standard gauge line with four stations, the contract price being £70,000 in fully paid up shares and £23,330 in debentures. This meant that, in effect, the contractor would acquire over £93,000 worth of shares and debentures, which he could (in theory) be able to sell at a profit. If, however, £7,500 worth of shares had not been subscribed for within a period of one calendar month the contractor would be able to withdraw from the arrangement.

After the letting of the contract, the next important step was the fixing of a date for the cutting of the first sod at Helston. It was at first decided that the event would take place in the 'Tile House Field' in Helston, the property of Mr F.V. Hill, on 8th March, 1882 but, because of 'unforeseen and unknown circumstances' this date was later considered to be unsuitable, and it was agreed that the ceremony would take place at the slightly later date of 22nd March, 1882.

Helstonians realized that, after many years of frustration and disappointment, the railway they wanted so badly was a distinct possibility, and they spared no effort to make the sod-cutting ceremony a success. Streets were to be decorated, trees planted, and triumphal arches erected; there would be a 'free tea' for all Sunday school scholars and 'old people over fifty', including the inmates of the Union Workhouse. Everyone worked enthusiastically, and a week before the 'appointed day' all the inhabitants were more or less engaged in assisting in the arrangements and sharing the enthusiasm which became more pronounced as the great day approached.

The cutting of the first sod took place, as arranged, in the Tile House Field on Wednesday 22nd March, 1882. It followed the pattern set on so many previous occasions throughout the country, and was the occasion for a great display of public enthusiasm. The town was be-flagged, trees were planted in the streets, and there were triumphal arches in Meneage Street, Wendron Street, Coinagehall Street, Church Street and Cross Street, all with appropriate mottoes. Most of the shops were closed in the afternoon and the occasion was deemed to be of such importance to the youth of the town that Thomas Taylor, headmaster of the Church of England school, recorded in the school log book: 'A whole holiday; cutting of the first sod of the Helston Railway'.

The event was originally considered important enough for the Prince of Wales to be invited to perform the opening ceremony. After all, his father the Prince Consort had opened the Royal Albert Bridge at Saltash on 2nd May, 1859, and the Prince himself had laid the foundation stone of Truro cathedral on 20th May, 1880; why then, should he not inaugurate the Helston Railway? (Local pride was probably somewhat hurt when this idea was dropped!)

An eyewitness account of 'Demonstration Day', written by William Roskilly to Edwin Richards of London, described in great detail the day's events - his letter being all the more remarkable in that it was 'written from memory, without the aid of notes, or reference to newspapers'. The 'Grocer's Apprentice' (as Mr Roskilly called himself), recalled how:

> From 8.00 am until noon, people flooded into the town by omnibus, carriage, phaetons, tricycles and what-not, one after the other and all together, and, in addition, a great number of pedestrians were also wending their way towards the Borough of Helston.

The *West Briton* newspaper reported that Helston had seen 'many days of gaiety and pleasure' when happy crowds thronged its granite streets, but 'the grandest Flora Day ever witnessed' had never brought 'such an assembly as

One of the triumphal arches erected in connection with the 'Cutting of the Sod' ceremony held at Helston on 22nd March, 1882; this example was set up in Coinagehall Street.
Oakwood Collection

was to be seen on this occasion'. In similar vein, *The Royal Cornwall Gazette* declared that 'the old town put on a thoroughly holiday appearance, the throng in the streets reminding one of the lively scenes enacted in these thoroughfares forty or fifty years ago, in the days when mining was at the height of its prosperity'.

As mid-day approached, the streets began to fill with people and vehicles, bands were arriving from various quarters, the Volunteers were marching, members of charitable societies were assembling in their full regalia, and the church bells began to ring. At one o'clock, the grand procession left the Bowling Green at the bottom of Coinagehall Street and, led by one of the bands, the diverse assemblage made its way through the town. Mr Alfred S. Oates, a well-known Helstonian, recorded in November 1955 (when he was 80 years of age) his impressions of the day's events. About six years old at the time, he had been placed on a wall to witness the march past of:

> The Mayor and Corporation. the county and town notables, bands, friendly societies with varied and extensive regalia; Oddfellows with large silvered representations of the sun, moon and. stars and much besides; Foresters on horseback with plumed feather hats, hunting horns and Robin Hood apparel.

A 'Demonstration Day' programme, now preserved in the Helston Folk Museum, reveals that, in addition to the various participants remembered by Mr Oates, the procession also included the 'constables and sergeants-at-mace', the 'Rational Society', the Helston Railway Directors, the shareholders and 'the committee'. At two o'clock the procession reached the Tile House Field at the north end of the town, and there, a vast crowd watched as the mayor of Helston, Richard Skews Martyn, turned the first sod and deftly placed it in a ceremonial wheel barrow; the bands then played the National Anthem and the first part of the sod-cutting celebration was brought to a close.

In the evening, Mr Oates recalled that he had been held shoulder high to see an electric light fixed on a high stand or scaffold where Lloyds Bank now stands; it was claimed that this display of light was 'the first ever in the county'. He also remembered that the silver spade and barrow used in the ceremony were carried in the procession by Mr W. Bassett.

Finally, there were spectacular firework displays in the lower part of the town, and a set piece entitled 'Success to the Helston Railway' was shown immediately in front of the Grylls Monument at the foot of Coinagehall Street (another set piece was called 'The Falls of Niagara', and this featured an appropriate cascade of fire in emulation of the famous water falls).

Preliminaries to construction

Land acquisition and other preliminary work continued throughout the early months of 1882, and with major construction work about to commence, the people of Helston and the surrounding area prepared themselves for an influx of navvies. The thought of armies of ill-disciplined labouring men descending on Helston was the cause of some alarm among certain property owners, and although railway navvies were probably much less fearsome than indigenous Cornish miners on a Saturday night, the local authorities decided to strengthen the local police force by appointing two extra constables. This precautionary measure did not pass unnoticed, and on 20th February, 1882 the *West Briton* printed the following, perhaps slightly humorous, paragraph:

> Helston is proverbially a quiet place, and for several years only one policeman and four elderly constables have been deemed by the Town Council sufficient. We have had no night police; at eleven pm it was concluded that all good citizens should be in their homes, and this has mostly been the case. Now, however, as the railway is to be commenced, and an influx of the dreaded navvies will invade us, the Council has issued a placard announcing that two additional constables will be employed. The candidates were to tender for the office. Six applicants sent in their tenders on Tuesday, and at the next meeting of the Council a selection will be made. No night police will be appointed, it being thought, by the majority of the Council, that the town is safe enough without them.

The authorized route, upon which the 'dreaded navvies' would soon be working, left its junction with the Great Western main line at Gwinear Road and, running south-eastwards, it then crossed an intervening ridge of higher ground before descending to Helston via the Cober Valley. By taking a more westerly course the work of construction would have been easier, but one assumes that problems with local landowners prevented this easier route from being adopted. The chosen route necessitated some considerable earthworks, and there would be one major viaduct across the Cober Valley near Helston, together with over 30 smaller overbridges, underbridges and underline culverts.

The exact site of Helston station was a particularly vexing question. It was originally suggested that the line should run from Gwinear Road, with stations at Praze, Nancegollan and Tregadjack Farm (for Wendron), and thence to Helston, crossing the Helston Road by a bridge 'near the nurseries' and terminating midway between the prison and the Union Workhouse. The site specified in the Act of Incorporation was generally considered to be less convenient, and after much adverse comment, the Helston Railway Directors held a meeting at the Angel Hotel in November 1881 in order that the question of the station site could be considered.

To the delight of the shareholders, the Secretary said that the Directors had met that very morning to discuss the matter, and they had agreed that the 'best and most convenient place for the station would be on the Beacon Garden, to the south of the workhouse, and between it and the prison. The additional cost consequent on the alteration of the site was £1,000, and it was proposed that this sum should be guaranteed by the Helston people'.

Several speakers opined that the proposed site would be the best, not only for the townsfolk, but for the while neighbourhood, and on the motion of Mr Bolitho the proposal was adopted unanimously. Sylvanus W. Jenkin, the Helston Railway Engineer, produced a set of plans to show the revised station site, and he stated that the GWR had agreed to seek Parliamentary consent for the proposed alterations in a general purpose Bill which they intended to promote in the forthcoming session.

At the end of 1881, the GWR duly deposited a Parliamentary Bill seeking (among other things), consent for:

A railway, commencing in the Parish of Wendron, in the County of Cornwall, by a junction with the authorized railway of the Helston Railway Company at or near the point marked 8 miles 2 furlongs on the plans deposited in respect of that railway with the Clerk of the Peace for the County of Cornwall in November 1879, such point being in the field numbered 6009 on the Tithe Commutation map of the Parish of Wendron, which field belongs to Frederick Vivian Hill, and is occupied by John Bray, and terminating in the Parish and Borough of Helston at a point about 38 yards to the southwards of the town prison, Helston, in a field belonging to Richard Kirby, and occupied by John Bray, which said intended railway will pass from, in, through or into the several parishes, townships, extra-parochial or other places, or some of them, viz - Helston and Wendron, in the County of Cornwall.

Another provision in the GWR General Purpose Bill related to the junction arrangements at Gwinear Road, where it was deemed necessary to obtain powers for another short section of new line, which was defined as:

A railway, to be wholly situate in the parish of Gwinear, in the County of Cornwall, commencing by a junction with the authorized railway of the Helston Railway Company at or near the point where such railway is intended to cross the road leading from the Company's Gwinear Road Station to Coswen Saussen Farm, such point being about 17 chains eastward of the entrance to the booking office of the said station, and terminating on the southern side of the railway of the Company on land belonging to the Company and adjoining their railway at a point thereon about 6 chains measured in a westerly direction from the entrance to the said booking office.

These measures were not in any way controversial, and they passed into law on 10th August, 1882, when the Great Western General Powers Act received the Royal Assent.

Construction begins

In May 1882 Sylvanus W. Jenkin reported that the arrangements 'for taking possession of the requisite land were, on the whole, in an advanced and satisfactory state'. Already, added the Engineer, 'a large quantity of plant' was either in position along the route of the line, or 'on its way down'. The works at Helston station had been commenced, and the terminus was 'actually in a state of active construction ... the contractor had arranged for a supply of a considerable quantity of fencing timber, and was expecting the wire' to be delivered in the very near future.

Work on the line was well under way by the summer of 1882, and on 2nd June the *Royal Cornwall Gazette* was able to report that the new railway works were in progress 'between Helston and the village of Lowerton, where a large viaduct is to be erected'. A few weeks later, on Friday 25th August, 1882, the same newspaper described the half-yearly meeting of the Helston Railway Company, which had been held on the previous Saturday:

HELSTON RAILWAY COMPANY – The half-yearly meeting of the shareholders in the Helston Railway was held in the Angel Hotel, Helston, on Saturday, Mr W. Bickford-Smith in the Chair. Among those present were Messrs W.M. St Aubyn MP, R.S. Martyn (Mayor of Helston), W. Bolitho Jnr, R.G. Rows, S.W. Jenkin (Liskeard) and F. Cartwright, Solicitor.

The directors reported that since the last meeting considerable progress had been made with the railway works, especially at the Helston end, and the contractor had been placed in possession of nearly all of the land required at both ends of the line. Proceedings for obtaining additional powers to enable the company to bring the Helston terminus into a more central part of the borough had been adopted in conjunction with the Great Western Railway, and the Bill had now obtained the Royal Assent. The directors would do their best to induce the contractor to press forward the works with all practicable expedition.

The report of the engineers stated that the works were in active progress, wire fencing had been fixed for a considerable distance, and a large portion of the wall at Clowance had been completed. About two thousand cubic yards had been excavated in cuttings and the foundations of the southern abutment and the piers of the Cober viaduct had been taken out. Occupation bridges had been built at various points, and important culverts completed; the company are in occupation of land required for six miles of line, and arrangements for a further portion are in a forward state. The accounts were passed, and the meeting concluded with the usual votes of thanks.

Unfortunately, subsequent progress was not as rapid as the Directors had anticipated, and at the beginning of 1883 the contract was suspended, the contractor being unable to carry on. The reason for this sad state of affairs were complex, though in retrospect it seems clear that Mr Maddison could not fulfil the onerous financial conditions that had been agreed between him and Helston Railway Company.

Examination of the Helston Railway minute book suggests that the contractor was unable to pay for the shares which would have partially financed the line, and which he had previously agreed to purchase. Under these circumstances, the money which should have paid the workmen was not forthcoming although, regrettably, Mr Relf, the principal sub-contractor, had 'laid out a great deal of money in speculation, hoping that Mr Maddison would have paid up'. There were, nevertheless attempts to continue the works under modified conditions, but in February 1883 Sylvanus W. Jenkin formally notified the Directors that 'Edward Charles Maddison the contractor of the railway, had failed to proceed with the works'.

In that same month, it was announced that the unfortunate Mr Relf, who had 'always been in advance with his work, and was looking forward to the completion of the line well within the prescribed time', had been obliged to lay off 'about 140 navvies and mechanics'.

On slightly lighter note, local newspaper reports referred to a 'disgraceful elopement' that had taken place when a discharged navvy known as 'Punch', who had been lodging with an old woman named Fanny Pike, ran off with Mrs Pike's 50 year-old married daughter, Mrs Trewin, the 'mother of 15 children', with whom he had been 'on very friendly terms'. On the day of the elopement, Mrs Trewin left home in company with several of her children with a jeering mob of neighbours in pursuit, while 'Punch' took the precaution of leaving much earlier, via a circuitous route, to avoid a posse of very angry relatives who had vowed to 'give him a thrashing'. The couple made their rendezvous later in the day in an ale-house at Crownton, and after taking some drink they made their way to Gwinear Road station and boarded the next train out of Cornwall.

The half-yearly shareholders' meeting held in Helston Town Hall on Wednesday 28th February, 1883 was a sombre gathering. William Bickford-Smith, in the chair, said that he was sure that all those present at the meeting would sympathise with the Directors in the unfortunate position in which they had been placed, but he thought that they had been 'careful and tolerably judicious' in every step that they had taken. He regretted that there had been a 'misunderstanding' between the contractor and sub-contractor which had led to the stoppage of the works, but he assured them that the matter had received the best attention of the Directors. The Chairman admitted that the project was not progressing smoothly, but his message to the proprietors remained optimistic:

> Since the last half-yearly meeting the work of construction was prosecuted with some activity up to the beginning of the present year when, to the great regret of the directors, and owing to circumstances over which they had no control, and into which it was not considered advisable to enter, the work was suspended. The shareholders may rest assured that every effort on the part of the directors will be made to secure the resumption of the works.

William Bickford-Smith and his fellow Directors were, at this stage, confident that the Great Western Railway would come to their rescue, but in practice the GWR was reluctant to spend its own money on a line which, when completed, would probably be no more than marginally profitable. In January 1883 two of the Helston Railway Directors had travelled to London in order to see James Grierson (1827-87) the Great Western's General Manager. Unfortunately, Mr Grierson was 'extremely busy' and, in an irritable mood, he tersely informed the Helston Railway representatives that it was 'not an auspicious time to come to the GWR Board to ask them to do anything to assist companies in making branch lines'. However, the GWR General Manager - realising, perhaps, that he may have been a little harsh - hinted that the Great Western might be prepared to help 'with regard to the guarantee of interest on debentures'.

Construction resumes

In the event, the GWR finally agreed to help the Helston railway in a number of ways, although there was, in the short term, no suggestion of any form of direct financial aid. Happily, the Helston Railway Directors were eventually able to secure the services of another contractor, and in February 1886 it was reported that Messrs Lang & Son of Liskeard were making good progress on the works between Gwinear Road and Helston. Construction was being rushed forward, and it was confidently predicted that the railway would be ready for opening by the following November. A few weeks previously, in October 1885, the steamship *Durley*, of Cardiff, had docked in Penzance with a cargo of 17,400 wooden sleepers for use on the new line.

The Directors were, it seems, delighted with the speed and efficiency with which Messrs Lang & Son had prosecuted the work, and the contractors were singled out for special praise at the half-year meeting held in the Guildhall at Helston on Saturday 15th March, 1886. They had, said the Directors, commenced work immediately, and had proceeded at different places with much vigour, the result being that on part of the line 'the permanent way had already been laid', while 'The masonry work was in an advanced state'. The half-yearly report then continued as follows:

> A matter which has given the directors much ground for consideration is the site of the station, a large number of the inhabitants of Helston being very desirous that the station should, if possible, be placed close to Meneage Street, and much thought has been given to the question as to whether or not this is practicable. The contract was taken by Messrs Lang on the understanding that the station and yard would be in the field where the sod was cut, commonly known as the Tile House Field, at the top of Wendron Street. To carry the station further would involve a rather heavy cost which the directors scarcely see their way to meeting, but they have the matter still under consideration to see whether it is practicable to meet the wishes of a large number of persons who will be using the railway most. The question is one that must soon be settled, as the contractors are desirous of laying out the station yard.

Having raised, the controversial matter of the station site - which had been much debated locally - the Directors looked back over the previous six months and, on this occasion, they were able to report that tangible progress had at last been made:

> Since the last half-year meeting the works on the line have been vigorously pushed on. A total of about 11,500 cubic yards of earthwork has now been taken out, and 7,200 cubic yards of masonry built. Out of a total of thirty-three bridges, five were built under the former contract, and nineteen more are either completed, or in course of construction, leaving nine to be built.
> At the Cober Viaduct arches Nos. Five and Six have been completed, and the centres have been removed from arch No. Six. Arches Nos. Two, Three and Four are in progress, and the centres are being fixed for arch No. One. The work on the viaduct has been somewhat delayed by the frost, but is now making satisfactory progress
> The line has practically been fenced throughout, and the contractors have been put in possession of nearly all of the land. The whole of the rails and sleepers required for the completion of the line have been delivered at Gwinear Road, and sufficient to lay about two miles of track have been carried out onto the line.

The half-yearly meeting ended with a question and answer session, and although few of the shareholders had actually turned up, there were some searching enquiries about the proposed station site at Helston. This was, clearly, still a highly-contentious issue and, in what may have been an attempt to stifle further discussion, Mr St. Aubyn, in the Chair, announced that the matter would ultimately depend upon the outcome of 'negotiations in London'. (In other words there was no money to bring the railway into Helston town centre, but it was possible that, with Great Western help, the existing plans could be altered.) Apparently satisfied with Mr St. Aubyn's explanation, the assembled proprietors then dispersed.

CONSTRUCTION, OPENING AND EARLY YEARS

The work of construction continued unabated throughout the summer of 1886, and with the major earthworks nearing completion, the Directors turned their attention to minor details such as the erection of stations and other buildings needed for the day-to-day operation of the railway. In theory, the design of each station was left in the hands of Sylvanus W. Jenkin who, acting in close liaison with Peter Margary (1820-96) the GWR Divisional Engineer, drew up the necessary plans. On 24th April, 1886, for example, Mr Jenkin attended a Helston Railway Board meeting, and the company minute book records that 'the plans of the of the stations at Gwinear Road and Helston were examined and approved'.

At a later meeting the Helston Railway Directors considered the provision of an engine shed at Helston, the original intention being that accommodation would be provided for two locomotives. However, the Great Western (which would, after all, be working the line) suggested that a somewhat smaller engine shed would be sufficient, and in August 1886 the Directors agreed that they would build 'a shed to take one engine instead of two', the money thus saved being expended on a retaining wall that was needed at Gwinear Road. At the same time, Mr Jenkin read a letter from his counterpart Mr Margary regarding the signalling and interlocking arrangements at the junction – all such matters being dealt with by the GWR. In reality, Peter Margary exercised a strong influence on all matters relating to track, signalling and architecture, and the design of Helston and the intermediate stations probably emanated from his own engineering department at Plymouth.

As the summer of 1886 turned inexorably to autumn, the Helston Railway began to take tangible shape in the remote Cornish countryside. Temporary contractor's railways had been used during the earliest stages of construction, horses being used to haul spoil wagons along the unfinished alignments. In a detailed report, published on Friday 17th September, 1886, the *Royal Cornwall Gazette* stated that:

> Rapid and satisfactory progress was being made with the new line of railway from Gwinear Road to Helston by the well-known contractors, Messrs Lang of Liskeard. The line will be nine miles in length, in which distance there will be no fewer than thirty-five bridges, including the Cober Viaduct. The permanent way has already been laid between six and seven miles, and it is anticipated that the remainder will be completed by the middle of October. The line is now being laid at the rate of ten chains, or one-eighth of a mile, per day. A locomotive is used to convey ballast during the day, and in the morning and evening carries sleepers, rails and the necessary fittings to the platelayers.
>
> The line is a single one, and the steel rails, which are of Vignoles section, weighing 75 lbs to the yard, are laid on transverse sleepers. The general curves of the line are remarkably light, the least being that of twelve chains at the viaduct. The gradients are also light, none exceeding one in sixty, and altogether it will be found to be a good running line, The engineer is Mr S.W. Jenkin of Liskeard, the resident engineer being Mr H. Hancock. At the present time Messrs Lang & Sons have about 300 men employed on the works, and at one time as many as close on 500 were engaged.
>
> The Helston passenger station is 300 yards from the turnpike, and will be approached by a roadway, 25 feet wide, now being made, the incline being one in twenty. The goods station will be on the eastern side, to which there will be a separate entrance by a road 20 feet wide, having an incline of one in twenty-five. Between these two roadways will be erected carriage sheds, 100 feet long, in which trains will be placed during the night.

The platform of the passenger station will be 300 feet long and built perfectly level. Advantage will be taken of the incline of the approach to the station to load travellers' trunks, boxes and luggage immediately from the platform, which will be on a level with the tops of omnibuses and cabs.

The passenger station will be commodious and convenient. In addition to the usual booking offices, waiting rooms, etc., there will be dining and refreshment rooms for the accommodation of the general public, and tourists in particular, it being anticipated that the line will be freely made use of by holiday seekers visiting the Lizard and the vicinity. The building itself will be of the most substantial character, and two-thirds of the masonry is already completed. The windows, doors and plinths are of fine picked granite and the walling of uncoursed fitted rubble masonry,

The goods sheds [sic] are 50 ft by 40 ft. There is to be made a long loading bank, similar to that at Marazion station, for the accommodation of vegetable and fish traffic. Immediately north of the passenger station at Helston stands the signal cabin, where the whole of the signal and switch arrangements will be under the control of one man. Nearby is a hot water apparatus for supplying foot warmers. About a hundred yards further north will be the engine shed, 40 ft by 20 ft, for the accommodation of locomotives.

The permanent way was, as predicted by the local press, in place by 1886, and on Saturday 30th October Mr Bickford-Smith and his fellow Directors were able to traverse the railway in a contractor's wagon that had been 'fitted up and placed at their disposal by Mr Lang'. This special excursion was, in effect, the first passenger train to travel over the branch. The up working left Helston at 9.45 am, carrying Mr Lang, his son, and their invited guests. The single-coach train stopped at Trevarno, about two miles from Helston, to pick-up William Bickford-Smith and his wife and children, after which the inaugural working continued to Gwinear Road. Here, the party was joined by Sylvanus W.Jenkin, Mr Molesworth St Aubyn MP, Mr Bolitho, and other Directors - Mr St Aubyn having arrived by main line train from Paddington, thereby becoming the first person to travel through from London to Helston by rail. After examining the newly-rebuilt junction facilities at Gwinear Road, the party returned to Helston, stopping intermediately at Praze and Nancegollan so that the Directors could admire the new stations. The train reached Helston around mid-day, having accomplished its outward journey in about half-an-hour, although the return journey had been a more leisurely affair.

Great Western engineers had, meanwhile, inspected the Helston line, and they were able to pronounce that progress had been much better than expected; indeed, the contractors had again been complimented for what they had achieved. This was most gratifying news, and in an atmosphere of renewed optimism the Helston Railway Directors suggested that additional capital might be raised in order to bring the new line nearer to Helston town centre - it being 'felt desirable to extend the line to the spot already mentioned to the public, near the Helston Union House, so as to bring a large share of business to the town'.

It was pointed out that the hoped-for extension could be built 'if some £3,000 worth of additional shares' were taken up, the Directors being responsible for the remaining £3,000. A contemporary report continued as follows:

CONSTRUCTION, OPENING AND EARLY YEARS

There is much interest manifested at Helston as to the locality of the railway station, and not a week remains for finally settling its whereabouts. The directors will willingly bring the line to the town instead of outside, provided the requisite amount of money can be procured. It appears that it will be necessary to get 150 twenty pound shares subscribed for in addition to the present capital. Some of these are already applied for, and there ought to be no difficulty in raising £3,000 when the importance of the question is understood. Really it means bringing the line into the centre of the borough instead of at an inconvenient distance outside the boundaries, and away from the town altogether.

Captain Rogers, RA, of Penrose, who holds a considerable number of paid-up shares, has not only offered to take additional shares, but will further increase his interest by taking shares in payment for all his land through which the extension will run. Other shareholders have promised to invest more money in the railway, provided the station is in Meneage Street. Public opinion is strongly in favour of bringing the railway to that point, and it is hoped that the directors will obtain the necessary support to warrant their going on with the work.

This again opened up the vexed question of the siting of Helston station, but the matter was finally settled when the additional capital required was not forthcoming, and Helstonians had to be satisfied with the Tile House Field site. Local opinion, however, remained strongly divided on the wisdom of choosing the Tile House Field as a site for the station, and, even as late as 1898, it was being argued that a site near the Union Workhouse would have been more accessible and convenient in every way.

An agreement with the GWR

In the meantime, the Helston Railway Directors had finalized their operating agreement with the Great Western, and after negotiation it was agreed that the GWR would provide the necessary locomotives and rolling stock. On 5th February, 1887 the *Railway Times* reported that the Great Western would work the line in return for 50 per cent of the gross receipts; this was in fact the usual arrangement, but the Helston company was able to secure a small advantage in that the Great Western agreed to pay rebates of five per cent on certain types of through traffic. Although the GWR could well afford this modest concession, the agreement was advantageous to the Helston Railway Company - which also obtained a financial safety net which would come into play in the event of that company's dividends falling below four per cent.

The suggested operating agreement was discussed at a Great Western general meeting held in February 1887, and in explaining it to his shareholders the GWR Chairman, Sir Daniel Gooch (1816-89) said a few words about the new Cornish branch line:

> The Helston Railway is a short branch from our line. It is an independent company, and we have agreed to work the line at 50 per cent, and we and the Cornwall Railway jointly agree to give a rebate on the traffic which comes to our line from theirs. I do not think there is much in the agreement to trouble about - it is very simple.

Having heard their Chairman's opinion, the rank and file Great Western shareholders readily agreed to this proposed operating agreement and, with the track and works at last nearing completion, the Helston Railway's supporters could, at long last, look forward to the opening of their railway.

The 'Dreaded Navvies'

Despite earlier fears of widespread public disorder as a result of the influx of several hundred navvies, the workmen involved in the construction of the Helston Railway caused little or no disruption to the local community. Indeed, there was unanimity of opinion that the navvies engaged by Mr Maddison and, subsequently, Messrs Lang & Son were, without exception, a body of 'well-behaved and inoffensive men'. Although the railway navvies drank prodigious amounts of alcohol, there were few arrests for drunkenness and no cases of assault on local people.

That is not to say that the work of construction proceeded entirely without incident and, notwithstanding what has been written elsewhere, the building of the Helston branch was not marked by a 'singular freedom from accidents'. On the contrary, accidents took place fairly frequently, and there are several references to these mishaps in the local press. On 13th November, 1885, for instance, the *Royal Cornwall Gazette* recorded, with a degree of understatement, a 'painful accident' that had befallen 'a lad called Manly, employed by Messrs Lang & Sons', who had been attending the boiler of a steam crane during the construction of the Cober viaduct, but missed his footing and fell about 30 ft to the ground, thereby breaking his thigh.

Shortly afterwards, the same newspaper mentioned that a navvy called Williams had 'received severe injuries' as a result of the collapse of an embankment that had been under construction at Gwinear Road. On Thursday 8th April, 1886 two navvies named Harper and Harris were injured by a fall of granite at Lowerton, Harper, who was from Liskeard, had his arm broken and his head badly cut, while Harris, who lived in Helston, received injuries to his face and head. A few weeks later, on 21st May, 1886, the *Royal Cornwall Gazette* described a similar accident that had taken place 'in the cutting at the Gwinear Road end of the Helston Railway' when a navvy called Richard Richards was fatally injured by a mass of earth which fell upon him and knocked him down, but did not bury him; the mortally-injured man was carried into 'a shed at the Gwinear Road station' but, sadly, he 'died after removal to Carn Brea'.

The Cober viaduct was the setting for a further incident on 29th September, 1886, when a navvy who rejoiced in the nick-name 'Navvy Bill' was working in a rock cutting on the Sithney side of the viaduct. He was engaged in boring a hole beside one that had miss-fired when the gunpowder exploded, throwing the drill that he was using high into the air and tearing his waistcoat from his body. Having sustained injuries to his arms and the side of his face, the lucky navvy was conveyed to Helston where his injuries were dressed by Mr Wearne, the local surgeon.

'Navvy Bill' appears to have had a fortunate escape, and in this respect his fate was much happier than that of Charles Shearman, a fellow-navvy who was paid-

CONSTRUCTION, OPENING AND EARLY YEARS

off from the works along with a group of fellow-workers on 17th July, 1886. With ample money in their pockets, the newly-discharged navvies retired to the nearest ale-house, from where, after a mammoth, day-long drinking session, they dispersed. Charles Shearman apparently decided to make his way to Wales but, having consumed a significant quantity of strong beer, he decided to spend the night in a convenient hayrick at Wheal Vor, near Sithney. This was to prove a fatal decision. At about 4 o'clock in the morning of 19th July, 1886, the sleeping navvy was discovered by the owner of the hayrick, Thomas Polglaze - a miner of notoriously 'morose disposition' who, according to his neighbours, 'was best left to himself'. For reasons that were not entirely clear, Polglaze smashed the navvy's skull with a 12 lb. peat-cutting axe, killing him instantly.

Having been charged with murder, Polglaze claimed that the sleeping navvy had been armed with a gun and would have killed him, but there seemed little doubt that the attack had been entirely unprovoked. Despite obvious doubts about his sanity, the accused man was sentenced to death, but the sentence was later commuted to penal servitude for life.

The Board of Trade report

The Helston branch was complete by the spring of 1887, but before their railway could be opened for public traffic the Directors had to arrange for the new line to be inspected by the Board of Trade (BoT). The necessary notification having been sent to the BoT, the inspection was arranged for the beginning of April, Colonel Francis H. Rich, RE, being appointed to inspect the route on behalf of the government. The detailed inspection took place as planned, and having examined the branch from end to end, the BoT Inspector produced a useful, first-hand account of the Helston Railway on the eve of its opening. His report, dated 6th April, 1887, is worth quoting in detail, some of the most interesting sections being as follows:

Sir,
I have the honour to report, for the information of the Board of Trade that, in compliance with the instructions contained in your minute of the 27th ultimo, I have inspected the new Helston Railway, which commences at Gwinear Road Station, on the West Cornwall section of the Great Western Railway, and ends at Helston.

The new line is 8 miles 68.89 chains long. It is single throughout, with sidings. The gauge is 4 ft 8½ inches, and the permanent way consists of steel rail of the Vignoles section that weighs seventy pounds per linear yard.

The rail is fished and fixed with long bolts to sleepers laid transversely about three feet apart, except those next to the rail joints, which are only about two feet apart. The sleepers are rectangular, 9 feet long by 10¼ inches. The line is well ballasted with broken stone and gravel, the ruling gradient is 1 in 60, and the sharpest curve has a radius of 9.09 chains.

The works consist of sixteen bridges over the railway which are built of stone, and two bridges for foot passengers that are constructed of wood. Fourteen bridges under the railway are built of stone, and four have stone abutments and wrought iron girders. There is a viaduct over the Cober consisting of six semi-circular stone arches of fifty feet span, which are carried on stone abutments and stone piers.

All of these works are very well and very substantially constructed. The wrought iron girders are strong by calculation, and gave moderate deflection when loaded. There is one authorised crossing of a public road at 9.25 chains from the commencement of the railway at Gwinear Road.

In general, the Board of Trade inspector was more than satisfied with the strength and stability of the newly-completed railway line, but at the same time he identified a few minor deficiencies which would have to be rectified prior to public opening. Most of these were of a trivial nature; the two timber foot bridges, for example, required 'two more rails at each side of the parapet' to 'prevent children from falling onto the railway', while two public foot paths that crossed the line on the level needed 'boarded paths' across the sleepers.

Another change demanded by the Board of Trade inspector concerned the principal intermediate station at Nancegollan, some 5 miles 9 chains from Gwinear Road. This had been laid-out as a potential crossing station with a second line that might, at some future date, be brought into use as a crossing loop. Colonel Rich was unhappy with this arrangement being sanctioned on a single track branch that would, for the foreseeable future, be worked as one section; he therefore ordered that Nancegollan should be 'altered to a one-sided station', the second road being used merely as a siding for goods traffic, rather than as a loop for crossing trains.

The proposed changes were evidently agreed-to by Sylvanus Jenkin during the inspection, and the Board of Trade inspector concluded his report as follows:

> The Company's Engineer has arranged for the arrangements to be completed, and I can recommend the Board of Trade to sanction the Helston Railway being opened for passenger traffic, subject to the usual undertaking as to the proposed mode of working being satisfactory.
>
> I have, etc.,
> F. Rich,
> Colonel RE

Having successfully passed its Board of Trade inspection, the Helston branch could be opened for public traffic, and the Directors decided that the official 'First Day' celebrations would take place on 9th May, 1887. This would be both a public opening and the official opening day - the idea being that the Board members and their invited guests would arrive at Helston station aboard a scheduled passenger train rather than on a special working.

Opening of the line

Opening day was treated as a public holiday in Helston and the surrounding area. The flags, bunting and other decorations that had been used in the sod-cutting ceremony were displayed once more, and the little town was *en fête* when the first up working steamed proudly out of the newly-built terminus on

CONSTRUCTION, OPENING AND EARLY YEARS 33

Monday 9th May, 1887. This first train, the 9.40 am to Gwinear Road, carried approximately 50 passengers, and its locomotive was adorned with flags and evergreens. The intermediate stations at Nancegollan and Praze were similarly adorned, and several local people turned out to see the inaugural working as it made its way along the line.

The Helston Railway directors travelled to Helston in a later train that left Gwinear Road at 12.50 pm. At Praze station, an address was officially presented by the Reverend J.W. Johns, the vicar of nearby Crowan, and at Nancegollan a group of additional passengers joined the Directors' special. The approach of the train to Helston was announced by loud cheering from schoolboys on the bridge near the station, and as the inaugural working into the platform, its triumphant arrival was accompanied by a veritable barrage of exploding detonators; the schoolboys were probably from the Church of England school, for the school's headmaster recorded in his log book: 'May 9th 1887, the Helston Railway from Gwinear Road opened today. Many boys absent. A half-holiday was granted'.

The train was met upon arrival at Helston by the Mayor and corporation, and as it steamed into the terminus the Helston Volunteer Band played *See the Conquering Hero Comes!*, this choice of music being highly appropriate in view of the many difficulties and disappointments that had, at long last, been overcome.

Greetings having been exchanged, the vicar, the Reverend Canon Tyack, offered a specially-composed prayer, and the Mayor read a formal address. William Bickford-Smith responded on behalf of the Helston Railway Company, and a photograph was taken in the forecourt of the station. The Mayor and corporation then joined the Directors for a round trip to Gwinear Road, and on their return at 3.10 pm the official party progressed to the Angel Hotel - where the Mayor presided over a luncheon 'provided at his expense'.

In addition to the usual loyal toasts, there were toasts to 'The Helston Railway', 'The Directors', and 'The Bishop, Clergy and Ministers of all Denominations'. These toasts were followed by a further toast to 'The Landowners' - each toast being preceded by a lengthy proposal and followed by an elaborate and wordy reply. In responding to the toast offered to the landowners, the Reverend St A.H.M. St Aubyn of Clowance spoke approvingly of the good behaviour of the navvies engaged upon the line.

Some details of the line

The newly-completed Helston line was, from its inception, worked by the Great Western Railway in return for 50 per cent of the gross receipts, as agreed prior to opening. The line was a standard gauge route and single track throughout, with no tunnels and only one viaduct - the Cober or Lowerton Viaduct near Helston. Situated just 1 mile 5 chains from Helston station, it had six arches and stood 90 ft above the valley at its highest point. Erected at a cost of £6,000, the viaduct was built of granite obtained from nearby rock cuttings and from a quarry only a few yards from the site.

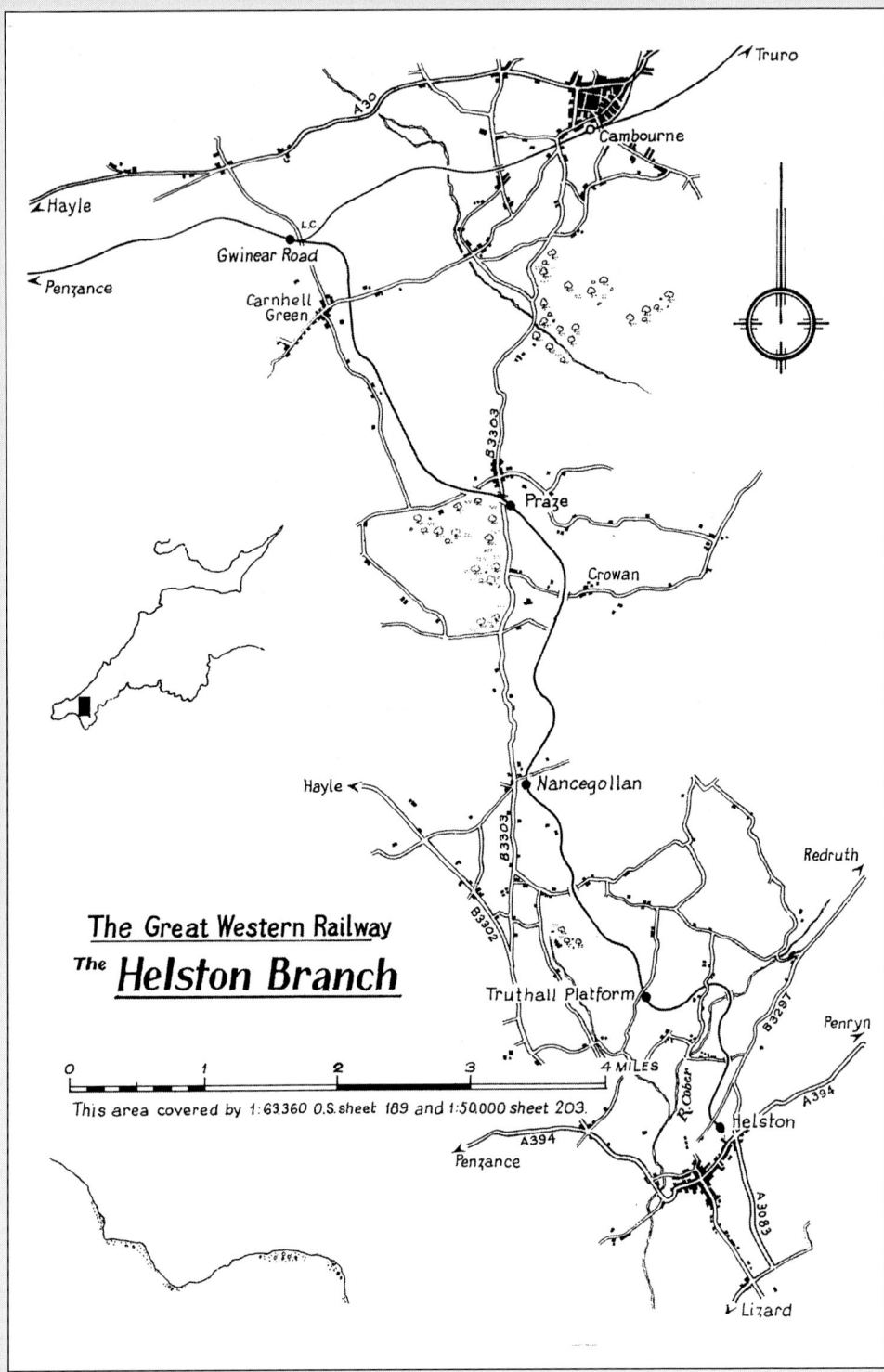

The branch commenced at a junction with the GWR main line at Gwinear Road station, ran east for a short distance, and then south-east and south for a total distance of 2 miles 68 chains over a ruling gradient of 1 in 60 (rising) before reaching Praze, the first station on the branch proper, in a running time of seven or eight minutes. From Praze to Nancegollan the line continued in a southerly direction for 2 miles 22 chains with a ruling gradient of 1 in 60 (falling), the running time being approximately six minutes.

From Nancegollan to Truthall the route became more steeply graded and more tightly curved; the distance of 1 mile 70 chains was over a falling gradient of 1 in 54 in a running time of six minutes.

Beyond Truthall the line took a sharp left-hand turn to the commencement of a horse-shoe bend which led to the Cober viaduct, just 62 chains beyond, and then to the last stretch of line, which gave a good run into Helston, 1 mile 5 chains distant, in a running time of six minutes, the gradient falling at 1 in 61. The line was 8 miles 76 chains in length from its junction at Gwinear Road to the end of the line at Helston, the distance shown in working timetables being 8 miles 67 chains, as the station at Helston was sited 9 chains (198 yards) short of the terminal buffer stops.

Although the Helston line was built at a relatively late date, it was a traditional rural branch; its buildings, for example, were solidly constructed of local stone, and in this respect the new line was more fortunate than certain other lines opened at around the same time. Shipston-on-Stour and Tetbury, for example, had simple wooden pre-fabricated buildings, which were in effect the Victorian equivalent of 'Portakabins'. Helston station was a squat, rectangular structure with a hipped roof and projecting platform canopy, while somewhat smaller, gable-roofed buildings were provided at the intermediate stations of Praze and Nancegollan. The locomotive shed was even more traditional (if that is possible) being a stone-built structure with a clerestory roof and arched entrance; similar buildings had been provided on Brunelian lines as far back as the 1850s.

As originally constructed, the branch had just two intermediate stopping places at Praze and Nancegollan, the idea of a third station at Tregadjack (for Wendron) having been quietly dropped. The two intermediate stations were of similar design, with loop sidings for goods traffic and single platforms for passenger traffic. Neither of these stations were passing places, but an intermediate crossing loop was subsequently installed about a quarter of a mile north of Nancegollan. A third stopping place was opened at Truthall in 1905, but this was no more than a halt, with rudimentary facilities for the occasional traveller.

Gwinear Road station was owned entirely by the GWR, though, to help the local company through its early years, the Helston Railway was allowed to use the junction facilities rent free for a period of seven years. All locomotives, rolling stock, tickets, waybills and other items necessary for day-to-day operation of the branch were provided by the Great Western under the terms of the operating agreement, while all train crews and other staff were GWR employees.

The Helston branch was, nevertheless a genuinely local railway, and its Chairman - William Bickford-Smith MP - lived locally, as did most of the directors; in 1890 these included William Bolitho (Deputy Chairman), Richard Skewes Martyn, Richard G. Rous, Walter Molesworth St Aubyn, David Wise Bain and the Reverend Sir Vyell Vyvyan, Bart. Most of these gentlemen seem to have been local landowners or professional people who had been associated with the railway from its inception. Collectively, they were some of the most important men in Cornwall, W. Molesworth St Aubyn, for example, being the former Member of Parliament for Helston, while Mr Bickford-Smith represented the newly-created Parliamentary constituency of Helston-Truro, which had been established under the provisions of the 1884 Franchise Act. Sylvanus W. Jenkin, the Helston Railway's Engineer, was also a local man, with roots in the Cornish peninsula; his birth place was at nearby Redruth, and he was also Engineer to the neighbouring Liskeard & Caradon Railway.

Early years of the Helston line

The newly-opened branch line was soon contributing to the economy of Helston and the surrounding area, the initial traffic returns being very encouraging. Receipts for the half-year ending December 1888 were £5,617 12s. 2d., a slight improvement over the corresponding period for June-December 1887.

Unfortunately, the local tin mining industry, which had been in severe decline since the 1870s, showed no sign of improvement during the 1880s. On the contrary, the industry continued to decline, with mines closing in increasing numbers. There were, in one or two places, desperate attempt to continue mining in the hope that trade would improve; at East Lovel Mine (to the north of Helston), it was reported that a productive lode had almost been reached, but the pumping engine had been 'stopped to reduce expenses' and the mine was 'almost flooded'.

It was clear that, in the Helston area at least, the tin mining industry was virtually finished, but there were, on the other hand, hopes that quarrying could provide employment for redundant tin miners - and also provide lucrative bulk traffic for the railway. In this context it is significant that, in 1886, the Coverack Stone Company had been formed to exploit the rich mineral resources around the Lizard coast. On 18th January, 1886, the *West Briton* reported that the company hoped to work 'on a very extensive scale' the quarries on the coast between Falmouth and the Lizard. The introduction of dynamite meant that, for the first time, the hard rocks that abounded in the Lizard area could be commercially quarried for roadstone and building and, although the Coverack company intended to export crushed stone aboard coastal vessels, other companies were expected to make use of the new railway for their transport needs.

Tourism was, like quarrying, a growth industry in late 19th century Cornwall, and the Helston Railway Directors had every reason to believe that their railway would be able to develop as a holiday line. As we have seen, the coastal villages of the Lizard peninsula were already popular among discerning tourists and holidaymakers, many of whom reached the area via Falmouth and the former Cornwall Railway route. By the 1880s, Cadgwith was being 'discovered' by increasing numbers of summer visitors, while Coverack was said to be 'filled' with lodgers for 'most of the summer'. It was a similar story at Porthoustock and Porthallow, which (claimed the *West Briton*) were 'slowly getting known'. The people who visited these watering places tended to be from the upper ranks of late Victorian society, but the provision of railways such as the Helston line ensured that large numbers of ordinary, middle class holidaymakers could also visit the Lizard and Meneage areas, and in the longer term the Helston branch was instrumental in placing villages such as Cadwith, Coverack and Mullion on the holidaymakers' map.

In 1892 the West Cornwall main line was converted to the standard gauge, and this brought further traffic to the Helston branch, as a result of the improved connections that were available at Gwinear Road.

The Helston branch was, of course, a standard gauge route from the time of its opening, but the narrowing of all GWR lines west of Exeter on the weekend of 20th-22nd May, 1892 brought disruption to all parts of the system. All broad gauge public services ceased on the evening of Friday 20th May, though Helston branch trains continued to operate on the following Saturday; there were, however, operational difficulties because three of the normal branch passenger vehicles had been temporarily transferred to the St Ives branch in order to work the first standard gauge trains between St Ives and St Erth on Monday 23rd May. The vehicles concerned were two ordinary thirds and a tri-composite, and their removal left very few coaches in service on the Helston line (this unsatisfactory situation was rectified when further standard gauge rolling stock was sent to Cornwall for use on the Helston, Falmouth and St Ives lines).

Disruption of a different kind occurred during the 'Great Blizzard' of March 1891 when Cornwall was affected by an unusually-severe snow storm, and the evening train from Gwinear Road to Helston became snowed-up in the cuttings between Praze and Nancegollan. Surrounded by 15 ft snow drifts, the locomotive became completely stuck, those aboard being forced to spend the night in the train. On the following morning the train crew and one passenger were able to reach the safety of a nearby farm. Towns such as Helston and Falmouth were, by this time, cut off from each other and from the outside world - the Cornish railway system having been blocked in numerous places by huge snow drifts.

The disruption lasted for almost a whole week and, in that time, the railway, postal and telegraph systems were paralysed. Sadly, the loss of all means of communication imperilled life at sea, insofar as it was virtually impossible to summon help for stricken vessels that had become trapped at various places around the treacherous Cornish coast. The worst loss of life occurred at Nare Point, when the four-masted steel sailing vessel *Bay of Panama* was driven ashore at the height of the tempest. Local rescue parties managed to save 17 seamen with the aid of a 'rocket apparatus and breeches buoy, but the master, his wife and 18 seamen were drowned. News of the disaster was brought to Helston by a man on horseback, but as the telegraph wires were down and the railway out of action he had to walk across country to Falmouth. On the way he encountered 'enormous difficulties', as reported in the *West Briton*:

Mullion Cove and Mullion Island, looking south-westwards, with the harbour visible in the foreground. Mullion was one of the many attractive places served by the GWR road motor services. *Author's Collection*

A general view of Cadgwith, a picturesque fishing village with two coves, which is situated on the east side of the Lizard Peninsula. *Author's Collection*

For a mile and a half or two miles he had to crawl along on his hands and knees through the snow. His face became coated with ice, and several times he had to break the ice from his eyes, whilst icicles hung from his ears. More dead than alive he came across a cottage in the occupation of a mason named Combellack. Here, he rested until daylight on Wednesday morning, when he resumed his journey and arrived in Falmouth at about nine o'clock.

Towards the end of the week the wind died down, and communications were slowly restored. The stranded engine was at last able to take its train of unheated carriages into Helston, and the branch was fully re-opened throughout its length on Saturday 14th March. The little town had been cut-off from Gwinear Road for almost a week, and the 200 men who had toiled to clear the line were welcomed by loud cheers when they finally entered Helston.

Blizzards notwithstanding, the inhabitants of Praze, Nancegollan and Helston enjoyed a comparatively good train service during the 1890s, and although the single track branch was worked as simply as possible on the 'one-engine-in-steam' system, there were around six or seven trains each way between Gwinear Road and Helston. In July 1894, for example, there were seven up and seven down workings, the first up train from Helston to Gwinear Road being at 8.12 am. At 8.50 am the branch train returned to Helston, and there were, thereafter, further round trips from Helston to Gwinear Road at 9.40 am, 11.50 am, 1.37, pm. 4.45 pm, 6.00 pm and 8.10 pm. In the reverse direction, the balancing down services departed from Gwinear Road at 10.35 am, 12.40 pm, 2.40 pm, 5.20 pm, 6.52 pm and 8.48 pm, respectively.

Week Days. HELSTON BRANCH.

DOWN TRAINS

Distance M | C	STATIONS	Passenger arr. | dep. A.M.	*Mixed arr. | dep. A.M.	Mixed arr. | dep. P.M.	Passenger arr. | dep. P.M.	Passenger arr. | dep. P.M.	Passenger arr. | dep. P.M.	Passenger arr. | dep. P.M.
— | —	Gwinear Road	— | 8 50	— | 10 35	— | 12 40	— | 2 40	— | 5 20	— | 6 52	— | 8 48
2 | 68	Praze	8 57 | 8 58	10 43 | 10 44	12 48 | 12 52	2 47 | 2 48	5 27 | 5 28	6 59 | 7 0	8 55 | 8 56
5 | 9	Nancegollan	9 3 | 9 4	10 50 | 10 51	12 58 | 1 2	2 53 | 2 54	5 33 | 5 34	7 5 | 7 6	9 1 | 9 2
8 | 67	Helston	9 15 | —	11 2 | —	1 13 | —	3 5 | —	5 45 | —	7 17 | —	9 13 | —

UP TRAINS

Distance M | C	STATIONS	Passenger arr. | dep. A.M.	Passenger arr. | dep. A.M.	Mixed arr. | dep. noon	†Mixed arr. | dep. A.M.	Passenger arr. | dep. P.M.	Passenger arr. | dep. P.M.	Passenger arr. | dep. P.M.
— | —	Helston	— | 8 12	— | 9 40	— | 11 50	— | 1 37	— | 4 45	— | 6 0	— | 8 10
3 | 58	Nancegollan	8 22 | 8 23	9 50 | 9 51	12 0 | 12 4	1 48 | 1 52	4 55 | 4 56	6 10 | 6 11	8 20 | 8 21
5 | 79	Praze	8 29 | 8 29	9 56 | 9 57	12 10 | 12 14	1 58 | 2 1	5 1 | 5 2	6 16 | 6 17	8 26 | 8 27
8 | 67	Gwinear Road	8 37 | —	10 5 | —	12 21 | —	2 10 | —	5 10 | —	6 25 | —	8 35 | —

NO SUNDAY TRAINS. The Helston Branch is a Single Line, worked by Train Staff.

No Block Telegraph. The Train Staff is a round one, painted black, and lettered "Gwinear Road and Helston" Only one Engine in Steam must be allowed to be on this Branch at one and the same time.

Until Further Notice the Block Telegraph between Helston and Gwinear Road will NOT be worked.

* Will convey Goods wagons, Gwinear Road to Helston only.

GWR working timetable, July 1894.

An early view showing Gwinear Road station from the level crossing, looking west towards Penzance, with the Helston branch platform visible to the left.
Lens of Sutton Collection

CONSTRUCTION, OPENING AND EARLY YEARS

The 11.50 am and 1.37 pm up trains and the 10.35 am and 12.40 pm down workings were mixed trains. Average journey times were 25 minutes for ordinary passenger workings, though the two up and two down mixed services were allowed a few minutes longer for the 8¾ mile journey. The line was, at that time, worked by train staff without the benefit of block telegraph, the train staff being round in section, painted black, and lettered 'Gwinear Road and Helston'.

The Helston Railway had been constructed to bring rail communication to the Helston area, and having accomplished their initial aims, the railway's promoters took little interest in the day-to-day operation of the line. Under these circumstances, the idea of an outright sale to the Great Western had many attractions, and in the middle-1890s the Helston Railway Directors agreed that their undertaking would be sold to the GWR. The line was formally vested in the Great Western Railway from 1st July, 1898, these arrangements being legalized by section 61 of a Great Western General Powers Act obtained on 2nd August, 1898.

The original Helston Railway £20 shares were purchased by the Great Western for £7 each, and this meant that some of the shareholders faced a financial loss. Local historian E.N. Cunnack has pointed out that the 'aim of the promoters was not immediate personal gain', and in retrospect the simple arithmetic outlined above would seem to prove that the supporters of the railway were interested primarily in 'service to the district at large'. Some of the shareholders undoubtedly profited from the provision of cheap transport for the area, while the farming community obviously welcomed the availability of rapid transport for perishable goods. On the other hand, the largest shareholders tended to be prominent landowners such as William Bickford-Smith and, as Mr Cunnack has suggested, such men gained very little in the short term. Their financial sacrifice was made, in great part, out of a sense of duty to the community, and without such men the railway (and others like it) would never have been built.

A rare view of GWR 0-4-4T No. 34 at the head of a branch train at Praze station.
Lens of Sutton Collection

A view from the turn of the 20th century of Helston station, looking towards the end of the line. the simple damond crossing on the right was removed in 1915, and thereafter engines reached the nearby engine shed by means of a connection facing to up trains. *Lens of Sutton Collection*

An interesting view of Helston station around 1904, showing some of the original flat-bottomed trackwork *in situ*; note the widely-spaced sleepers, which were placed about 3 ft apart.
Lens of Sutton Collection

CONSTRUCTION, OPENING AND EARLY YEARS

The Helston railway promoters - A further note

Cornwall is a small, circumscribed area, surrounded by the sea on three sides and virtually an island. In these circumstances the local gentry were a small, tightly-knit group, and it is hardly surprising that the same family names featured, time and time again, as the promoters of local railways. The St Aubyns, for example, were represented on the Boards of the Helston Railway, and the abortive Helston & Penryn scheme, John St Aubyn being a director of the Helston & Penryn Junction Railway, while W. Molesworth St Aubyn sat on the board of the Helston Railway; both were related to the St Aubyns of St Michael's Mount.

The Bassets and Vyvyans were similarly involved in a number of local railway projects, and Thomas Agar Robartes (later Baron Robartes of Lanhydrock) was an active supporter of railways and other new developments throughout his native county. Sadly, Lord Robartes died in 1882, and although he had featured prominently in the Helston & Penryn scheme, he did not live long enough to participate in the Helston Railway project. There was, nevertheless a link between Lord Robartes of Lanhydrock and the Helston branch, insofar as Thomas Lang, the contractor who had carried out such excellent work on the line, had spent about four years rebuilding Lanhydrock House after a major fire in 1881. Messrs Lang & Son thereby became well-known as reliable building firm, and it was, perhaps, no coincidence that they were later selected as contractors for the gentry-dominated Helston Railway Co.

Another point which might be made in relation to Cornish landowners such as the St Aubyns, Bassets and Agar Robartes, is that they were heavily-involved with the local tin-mining industry, either as active mine owners or (more usually) as 'Mineral Lords'. Mines with names such as Wheal Vyvyen, West Basset and Wheal Agar underline the links that existed between tin mining and the local gentry, and explain - at least in part - why the landowning classes were such enthusiastic supporters of railway schemes such as the Helston & Penryn Junction project.

When, from the 1870s onwards, the mines went into decline, those same landowners sought to alleviate unemployment by initiating 'job creation programmes'. In October 1878, for example, the *West Briton* reported that several landowners - among them Lord Robartes at Wendron and William Bickford-Smith at Helston - were having tracts of waste land broken-up for cultivation in order 'to find employment for the superabundant labour in Cornwall'; in this context railways were themselves seen as ways of stimulating economic development, and the Helston Railway was clearly planned as an adjunct to improvements in the fishing, farming and quarrying industries.

The Lizard Light Railway

As the 19th century drew to a close, there was much talk of a light railway from Helston to the Lizard, and indeed, in March 1898 the Board of Trade issued a Light Railway Order authorizing the construction of 'A Light Railway in the county of Cornwall from the Helston Railway to the Lizard Village'. Further details of the proposed light railway scheme appeared in the *Royal Cornwall Gazette* on Friday 2nd March, 1898:

The order, which bears upon it the name of Mr J. Walter Tyacke, of Helston, as the solicitor to the promoters, provides for the incorporation of several necessary Acts of Parliament, and gives to Archibald Edward Scot, Pearce Jenkin, Samuel Thornely Mote and other persons the right of uniting in a company for the purpose of making and maintaining the railway. It directs that the number of directors shall not be less than three nor more than five, the qualification to be twenty-five shares.

The railway is to be eleven miles, two furlongs and nine chains in length, commencing in the Borough of Helston by a junction with the Helston Railway and terminating in the parish of Landwednack. It is to be on a gauge of four feet eight and a half inches, and the motive power is to be steam or such other power as the Board of Trade may approve. The powers for the compulsory purchase of lands are to cease after three years, and the Order provides certain restrictions on the taking of an undue number of houses of the labouring classes for the purposes of the railway. If the railway is not completed within five years the Board of Trade has power to extend the time, or order the work uncompleted to cease.

The bridges over public highways authorized to be carried over the highways are one in Helston, one in Wendron and two each in Mawgan and Mullion. The alteration of roads which, howeverhave to be properly restored and maintained for twelve months, after which they are to be handed over to the public authorities. There are several clauses for the protection of the Great Western Railway. One provides for the junction at Helston being made in accordance with such plans as the principal engineer of the Great Western Railway may approve, the Light Railway Company to pay the cost of the rearrangement of the lines of railway and sidings of the Helston Railway and the removal of the existing goods shed at Helston and its re-erection on another site, and of the construction of an additional passenger platform at that station so as to make it a double platform station with a footbridge connecting the two platforms, a crossing place for trains, and of any other works required. Provision is made for the proper inspection of the new railway by an officer of the Board of Trade under severe penalties.

Accommodation is to be made for three stations, one at Dodson's Gap, two miles from Helston, one near Trevassack, five miles from Helston, and one near Penhale, seven and a half miles, and one at the termination of the railway near the Lizard village. No train is to be run at any time at a speed exceeding twenty-five miles an hour. The company is authorized to enter into agreements with the Great Western Railway Company for the maintenance and management of the railway, the working of it, the collection, transmission or delivery or traffic, the fixing of rates and charges, the supply and maintenance of rolling stock, and the employment of officers and servants. There is a clause protecting the Postmaster-General in regard to the telegraph wires and works, and there are voluminous regulations inserted in case the company decide to use electric motive power.

A scale is also provided for the charges for carrying small parcels on the railway, the maximum for which is nine pence for fifty-six pounds ... The capital of the Company is to be £75,000 in 7,500 shares of £10. The company may from time to time borrow on mortgage any sum not exceeding £25,000 in respect of each £25,000 of the capital, under certain stipulations as regards the amount paid upon the shares; and no mortgagee can make an application for the appointment of a receiver until the amount owing to him is £2,000. Debenture stock is also authorized. The order is issued subject to the provisions of the Light Railways Act, and it is laid down that certain matters shall in case of dispute be referred to arbitration. There is a schedule attached to the Order, which provides, among other details, that the rails shall weigh at least 60 lbs per yard. There is to be no obligation on the company to provide shelter or conveniences at any station or stopping place.

In the event, the proposed Lizard Light Railway scheme was overtaken by events. The Great Western, having taken over the Helston Railway Company, showed little interest in the idea of spending £80,000 on the construction of a branch line in sparsely-populated countryside that offered little scope for traffic development.

Chapter Three

The Line in Operation

Train services on the Helston branch were modest in comparison with certain other seaside lines, and there were typically about eight or nine passenger workings each way between Gwinear Road and Helston. In 1909 for instance, there were nine up and nine down trains, while in October 1920 the basic off-season timetable provided eight workings each way. The normal weekday train service was augmented during the period of the summer timetable by four or five additional trains on Saturdays. Additional trains were also run to arrive at Helston early on Christmas morning, to cater for those travelling by the extra night trains from London on Christmas Eve.

The line was (by 1920) worked on the electric train staff system, with signal boxes at Gwinear Road, Helston and at Nancegollan Loop near Nancegollan station. Nancegollan loop, opened in 1908, was the only intermediate passing place on the branch, but it was necessary to cross only one or two trains daily. Accidents, serious breakdowns or derailments were rare, but on occasions there was a failure of the staff instrument when the signalman at Helston was unable to obtain the staff from the instrument, and the train would be delayed until a pilotman arrived.

Operation in the early 20th century

In October 1920 the daily train service began with an early morning departure from Helston at 6.40 am. This working reached Gwinear Road by 7.05 am, and returned to Helston at 7.20 am. There was another round trip to Gwinear Road at 7.55 am, and then at 9.45 am the branch train set off for the junction once again; the balancing working from Gwinear Road to Helston was a mixed formation which conveyed incoming freight vehicles.

At 11.55 am the locomotive and passenger stock returned to Gwinear Road from where, at 1.05 pm, there was another mixed working back to Helston. Thereafter, the branch train made a round trip to Gwinear Road, leaving Helston at 1.45 pm and arriving back by 2.57 pm. Meanwhile, a goods train had left Helston at 2.10 pm; this reached Gwinear Road at 3.17 pm, having passed the returning passenger train in Nancegollan Loop. This operation was repeated at 4.14 pm when the 3.50 pm goods from Gwinear Road crossed the 4.00 pm passenger service from Helston; the passenger train returned from Gwinear Road at 5.05 pm, and the day's train service ended with two more round trips from Helston to the junction.

There were no Sunday trains in 1920, and indeed regular Sunday train services never became an established feature of Helston branch operations (although bus services were advertised on the Helston to Gwinear Road route).

In contrast to many other Cornish branch lines, the Helston route was not served by summer Saturday through workings to and from Paddington. There

HELSTON BRANCH.

Single Line worked by Electric Train Staff between Helston and Gwinear Road. Crossing Places, Helston, Nancegollan Loop and Gwinear Road.

Week Days only.

Distance		Station No.	STATIONS.	Ruling gradient 1 in	Time allowances for Ordinary Freight Trains. See page 2.			1	2	3		4	5	6		7	8		9		10		11		12	13	14
								Passenger.	Passenger.	Mixed.		Passenger.	Mixed.	Passenger.		Passenger.	Goods.		Passenger.		Passenger.		Passenger.		Passenger.		Passenger.
					Point to point times.	Allow for stop.	Allow for start.	dep.	arr. dep.	arr. dep.		dep.	dep.	arr. dep.		arr. dep.	arr. dep.		arr. dep.		arr. dep.		arr. dep.		dep.		dep.
M.	C.				Mins.	Mins.	Mins.	A.M.	A.M. A.M.	A.M. A.M.		A.M.	P.M.	P.M. P.M.		P.M. P.M.	P.M. P.M.		P.M. P.M.		P.M. P.M.		P.M. P.M.		P.M.		P.M.
—	—	9085	Gwinear Road	—	—	—	—	7 20	— 8 30	— 11 25		1 8	—	2 30		— 3 30	4 6		5		— 6		— 6 23		—		8 0
2	05	2231	Fraze	60 R	8	1	1	7 28	— 8 38	11 28 11 30		1 13	—	2 38		3 14	4 14		5 6		6 4						8 7
4	62	2232	Nancegollan Loop	57 F	6	1	1	CS CS	CS CS	CS		CS	1 20	CS CS		CS CS	CS CS		CS		CS		CS		CS		CS
5	0	2233	Truthall Platform	60 F	6	1	1	7 34	9 9	11 42		1 27	1 27	2 45		4 20	4 20		5 11		6 13		6 30				8 14
7	0	2234	Helston Stop Board	61 R	—	—	—	—	9 10	11 46		—	P	2 52		4 23	4 62		—		—		—				—
8	67	2235	Helston	61 B	10	—	—	7 45	9 15	11 52		1 31	P	2 57		4 29	4 20		5 20		6 20		6 40				8 25

Distance		Station No.	STATIONS.	Ruling gradient 1 in	Time allowances for Ordinary Freight Trains. See page 2.			1	2	3	4	5	6	7		8	9		10	11	12	13	14
								Passenger.	Passenger.	Passenger.	Passenger.	Passenger.	Passenger.	Passenger.		Goods.	Passenger.		Mixed.	Mixed.	Mixed.		
					Point to point times.	Allow for stop.	Allow for start.	arr. dep.	arr. dep.	arr. dep.	arr. dep.	dep.	arr. dep.	arr. dep.		arr. dep.	dep.		dep.	arr. dep.	arr. dep.		
M.	C.				Mins.	Mins.	Mins.	A.M.	A.M.	A.M. A.M.	A.M. A.M.	A.M.	P.M. P.M.	P.M. P.M.		P.M. P.M.	P.M.		P.M.	P.M. P.M.	P.M. P.M.		
—	—		Helston	—	—	—	—	6 10	—	7 35	9 35 11 35	12 2	1 55	2 40X 3 22		2 50 3 46	4 0		4 14	5 30 5 47	6 50 6 57		
1	67		Truthall Platform	61 R	1	1	1	—	—	8 2	9 50 12 2	12 9	CS	2 40X		3 11P 4 13	4 14		CS	CS CS	CS		
3	58		Nancegollan	65 R	10	1	1	CS	CS	CS CS	CS CS	CS	CS	CS		CS CS	CS		CS	CS	CS 7 4		
4	6		Nancegollan Loop	60 R	—	—	—	6 61	6 61	8 8	10 2 12 15	12 16	2 1	2 46		3 17P	4 20		4 23	5 64	6 64		
6	79		Fraze	57 R	6	1	1	6 67	6 67	8 14	10 8 12 16	—	2 7	2 60		—	—		—	6	6		
7	7		Gwinear Rd. Stop Board	60 F	6	—	—	—	—	—	—	—	—	—		—	—		—	—	—		
8	67		Gwinear Road	61 F	2	—	—	7 5	7 6	8 23	10 10 12 23		2 10	3 17		4 30	4 30		4 30	6 8	7 10		

* To convey Broccoli traffic from Helston only.

† For **ST** work only.

‡ All Trains not booked to call at Nancegollan and Fraze for traffic purposes must stop dead at those Stations to comply with No. 6 Appendix to Service Book.

Truthall Halt.—Trains timed to call at this Halt will not do so unless there are passengers to alight of entrain. The Station Masters at Nancegollan and Helston will arrange for each train to be examined, and if there are no passengers for Truthall Halt, the Guard and Driver must be instructed not to call at that place unless the Driver observes passengers at the Halt waiting to proceed.

Great Western Railway working timetable, October, 1920.

Commenced November 1st.

7.0 a.m. Carn Brea Yard to Helston.

	arr. a.m.	dep. a.m.		arr. a.m.	dep. a.m.
Carn Brea Yard ...	—	8 0	Nancegollan Loop ...	C S	
Gwinear Road ...	8 15	9 10	Nancegollan ...	9 23	9 35
Praze	C R		Helston	9 47	—

2.25 p.m. Helston to Carn Brea Yard.

	arr. p.m.	dep. p.m.		arr. p.m.	dep. p.m.
Helston	—	3 42	Gwinear Road ...	4 22	4 45
Nancegollan	3 54	4 2	Camborne	4 53 ●	5 22
Nancegollan Loop ...	C S		Dolcoath	5 27 ●	5 50
Praze	4 9	4 14	Carn Brea Yard ...	5 55	—
Gwinear Road S.B. ...	P	—			

Commenced January 2nd.

An undated timetable (probably around 1910) for goods traffic on the Helston branch.

GWINEAR ROAD and HELSTON (1st and 3rd class)

Miles	Down.	Week Days. mrn	mrn	mrn	aft	aft	m	aft	aft	aft		Sundays. mrn	aft	
	Gwinear Road...dep.	7 10	8 55	1040	1245	3 15	4 50	5 20	6 55	9 20	....	7 10	5 35	....
2¾	Praze	7 18	9 2	1047	1252	3 23	4 58	5 28	7 3	9 23	....	r	r	....
5	Nancegollan	7 24	9 8	1054	1259	3 29	5 4	5 34	7 9	9 34	....	7 50	6 15	....
7	Truthall Platform....	....	9 16	....	1 6	....	....	5 40	7 15	....	....	....	....	....
8¾	Helston ‖........arr.	7 35	9 24	11 5	1 14	3 40	5 15	5 48	7 22	9 45	....	8 20	6 45	....

Miles	Up.	Week Days. mrn	mrn	mrn	mrn	aft	aft	m	aft	aft		Sundays. mrn	aft	
	Helston.........dep.	6 30	7 55	9 50	1155	1 55	4 10	5 55	6 20	8 35	....	5 45	4 10	....
1¾	Truthall Platform..	....	8 0	....	12 0	....	4 15	....	6 27	8 40	....	r	r	....
3¾	Nancegollan	6 41	8 8	10 1	12 8	2 5	4 23	6 6	6 34	8 48	....	6 11	4 36	....
6	Praze ....[27	6 47	8 14	10 7	1214	2 12	4 29	6 12	6 40	8 54	....	....	....	....
8¾	Gwinear Road. 22,	6 55	8 22	1015	1222	2 21	4 38	6 20	6 48	9 2	....	6 55	5 20	....

m Motor Car, one class only. r By Road Motor.

‖ Station for Porthleven (2¾ miles), Mullion (6 miles), The Lizard (10 miles), Kynance Cove (10 miles), Housel Bay (10½ miles), Cadgwith (9½ miles), and Coverack and St. Keverne (10½ miles).

The Lizard.—Road Motors leave Helston Station at 7 45 and 11 15 mrn., and 5 25 aft. for the Lizard. Cars also leave the Lizard at 8 20 mrn., 2 45 and 4 15 aft. for Helston Station.

Bradshaw's Timetables, April 1910 (*above*) and July 1922 (*below*).

GWINEAR ROAD and HELSTON.—Great Western.

Miles	Down.	Week Days only. mrn	mrn	mrn	aft	aft	aft	aft	aft
	Gwinear Road.........dep.	7 10	8 50	1110	1 0	2 35	4 55	6 5	8 0
2¾	Praze	7 18	8 58	1118	1 8	2 43	5 3	6 13	8 8
5	Nancegollan	7 24	9 4	1125	1 15	2 51	5 9	6 19	8 15
7	Truthall Platform	....	9 10	....	1 21	2 57	....	6 25	8 21
8¾	Helston § ....arr.	7 35	9 15	1137	1 26	3 2	5 20	6 30	8 26

Miles	Up.	Week Days only. mrn	mrn	mrn	mrn	aft	aft	aft	aft
	Helston................dep.	6 30	7 55	9 45	1155	1 45	3 55	5 25	6 55
1¾	Truthall Platform..........	....	8 2	....	12 2	....	4 2	5 32	7 2
3¾	Nancegollan	6 41	8 9	9 56	12 9	1 56	4 9	5 39	7 9
6	Praze	6 47	8 15	10 2	1215	2 2	4 17	5 45	7 15
8¾	Gwinear Road 22, 27..arr.	6 55	8 23	1010	1223	2 10	4 25	5 53	7 23

A Service of Road Motors runs between Helston Station
miles), Mullion (6 miles), The Lizard (10 miles), Kynance Cove (10
and Porthleven and between Helston Station and The Lizard.

§ Station for Porthleven (2¾ miles), Mullion (6 miles), The Lizard (10 miles), Kynance Cove (10 miles), Housel Bay (10½ miles), Cadgwith (9½ miles), and Coverack and St. Keverne (10½ miles).

Gwinear Road station, looking east towards Paddington in the Edwardian period, *circa* 1910, and showing the up and down platforms, station buildings and level crossing. The main line platforms here were 578 ft long, while the branch platform had a length of 540 ft.
Lens of Sutton Collection

An Edwardian scene at Helston station, *circa* 1910, showing the single platform and station buildings, looking north towards Gwinear Road. 'Mink' vans and sheeted opens occupy the goods sidings, while 70 lb per yard flat-bottomed trackwork is still much in evidence.
Lens of Sutton Collection

were, perhaps two reasons for this omission. Firstly, the junction at Gwinear Road was aligned towards Penzance rather than towards London, and this meant that through trains would be faced with a time-consuming reversal before they could enter or leave the branch. However, of even greater significance was the fact that Helston was not actually by the sea, and although the branch carried a considerable number of holidaymakers, it was never as popular as 'true' seaside lines such as the neighbouring St Ives or Falmouth branches. If the Helston route had ever been extended to the Lizard the Great Western would probably have introduced at least some through coaches - there might, for example, have been a Helston coach in the formation of the Cornish Riviera Express, but in the event the Helston route remained one of the few Cornish branch lines that was never served by the Great Western's most famous named train.

Mention of the Cornish Riviera serves, however, as reminder that the afternoon train from Helston to Gwinear Road was traditionally known locally as 'The Riviera'. This appellation was, to some extent, in the nature of a joke, though the train in question did indeed connect with the Cornish Riviera Express at Gwinear Road - giving through travellers a reasonable journey time between Paddington and stations to Helston.

The Helston branch was originally worked by small Great Western tank locomotives, notably the '850' class 0-6-0 saddle tanks, which were widely used on the route during the late Victorian period. Some examples known to have worked on the line during the 1890s included Nos. 859, 992, 1935, 1943 and 1973.

The most distinctive locomotives seen on the Gwinear Road to Helston line in the early years of the 20th century were two picturesque and curiously-elongated 0-4-4Ts that had been built at Swindon specifically for use on short feeder branches. Carrying the numbers 34 and 35, these two small tank engines were alternated between the St Ives and Helston lines, but it appears that they were not particularly successful, and the design was not perpetuated.

Four-coupled 0-4-2T locomotives of the '517' class were also used on the Helston branch, some random examples being Nos. 569, 831, 1158, 1163 and 1481, all of which were stationed in the West Cornwall area and appeared on the route around 1920. Another four-coupled type used on the line were the 'Metro' class 2-4-0Ts - a venerable class that had been introduced in 1869 for service on the Great Western London suburban trains; they also worked over Metropolitan Railway lines. By the 1930s, the surviving 'Metro' 2-4-0Ts had become widely-dispersed throughout the Great Western system, and in August 1933 R.W. Kidner recorded an unidentified member of the class at work on the Helston route. In January 1935 it is recorded that 'Metro' No.1496 was allocated to Helston, while sister engine No. 3582 was employed on the branch in 1938.

In 1904 the Great Western constructed a prototype 2-6-2 side tank locomotive with outside cylinders and 4 ft 1½ in. coupled wheels. Ten similar engines emerged from Wolverhampton Works in 1905. These 11 locomotives - which subsequently became the '44XX' class - were intended for use on steeply-graded branch lines, their large boilers, short coupled wheelbase and small wheels making them ideally-suited for use on Cornish routes such as the Helston and St Ives branch lines. The first small prairie to appear in West

Cornwall was No. 3103 (later 4403), which arrived in February 1906 from Wolverhampton works, and started work on the St Ives branch. In the next few years, the '44XX' class 2-6-2Ts were widely used on the local branch lines, Nos. 4401, 4403, 4405, 4406, 4408 and 4409 being among those used in the area at various times between 1906 and 1925.

The '44XX' class engines were later joined by the visually-similar, but slightly larger '45XX' class prairies, which had arrived in West Cornwall in considerable strength by the 1930s, and eventually replaced the '44XX' class on local branch line duties. The '45XX' small prairies soon became well-established in West Cornwall, and it would probably be true that in the eyes of most enthusiasts, they were the Cornish branch line engines *par excellence*. The small prairies were classified as 'Yellow' engines under the GWR weight restriction system, and this ensured that they could work on all of the Cornish branch lines.

The branch locomotives were sub-shedded at Helston, a single-road locomotive shed being provided for that purpose. There was, on the other hand, no turntable, and for this reason the branch engines ran chimney-first on up journeys to Gwinear Road. Helston was a sub-shed of Penzance, and the normal branch engine was returned periodically to its home depot for routine maintenance operations. Additional locomotives were supplied by Penzance during the course of the day's operations, while the pattern of services provided on the line ensured that two or three engines were needed to work the route at any one time.

It is interesting to note that, during the early years of the 20th century, steam railmotors were apparently seen on the Helston route. The 1910 timetable, for example, reveals that the 4.50 pm service from Gwinear Road and the 5.55 pm return working from Helston were worked by one of these self-propelled vehicles.

Excursions & Tourist Traffic

One of two occasions during the year, especially before World War I, were red letter days for Sunday school children. A special train of six or seven coaches would be provided for the annual outing to Carbis Bay, on the neighbouring St Ives branch, and hundreds of children, with their parents and teachers, would travel on what, to many of them, was the only rail journey, and the only outing, that they would have made during the year. It was noticeable that the attendance at Sunday school was always good for at least a month before the trip in order to make the necessary number of attendances to qualify for a free outing. Such was the importance of the occasion, and such the understanding between the railway officials at Helston and the townspeople, that it was not unknown for the departure time to be delayed for a few moments, if necessary, to allow the older people time to walk to the station without having to hurry unduly over the last 100 yards or so. The weather for these trips was nearly always fine, only one case being recollected when the weather was bad, and that was nearly at the end of the day when passengers were waiting at Carbis Bay for the return train.

THE LINE IN OPERATION

In the 1920s, and up to the beginning of World War II, the Cornish tourist industry continued to develop rapidly, and the normal passenger traffic was augmented considerably on Fridays and Saturdays during the summer holiday period between June and September, when large numbers of people travelled to Helston for their annual holiday in the coastal villages of the Lizard peninsula. The branch was particularly busy on 'Flora Day', 8th May, and on 'Plum' or 'Harvest Fair' day (usually the first Monday in September) when additional trains were run to cater for hundreds of extra travellers.

The Lizard Road Motor Services

It will be remembered that the promoters had, in 1879, envisaged that the railway might, 'at some future date', be extended southwards to the Lizard and other adjacent districts, and indeed at Helston the running line projected beyond the platform for a considerable distance in order to facilitate such an extension. This idea had not been lost sight of, and indeed, at one time it was hoped that the Lizard 'might become the 'Torquay of Cornwall'. There was even a possibility of the hoped-for extension being built under the provisions of the Light Railways Act at an estimated cost of £80,000, but the proposal was not proceeded with, and the scheme was eventually abandoned. Instead, the Great Western Railway, always a pioneer, introduced a 'road motor' omnibus service from Helston station to Mullion and the Lizard on 17th August, 1903, thereby opening up the whole of the Lizard district to tourist traffic - to the great advantage of the hotel and boarding housekeepers.

In 1890 the Belfast & Northern Counties Railway (B&NCR) had introduced a petrol-engined van which (though intended for parcels delivery) was also fitted with passenger seats, and in 1903 the narrow gauge Lynton & Barnstaple Railway (L&BR) had purchased two similar vehicles for use between Ilfracombe and Blackmoor Gate station. The L&BR buses were Milnes-Daimler vehicles, and for legal reasons they were owned, not by the L&BR, but by a subsidiary company that had been formed by Sir George Newnes, the Lynton & Barnstaple Chairman.

The L&BR motor buses were allowed to operate for about five weeks but, sadly, local landowners objected to the radical new vehicles, and as these gentlemen happened to be magistrates they were able to inflict punitive fines for excessive speed when one of the buses was found to be travelling at over eight mph on a public road! Understandably angry at such blatant victimization, the L&BR sold its two buses to the GWR, and these ex-Lynton & Barnstaple motor buses were used to inaugurate the first GWR road motor service between Helston station and the Lizard in August 1903.

Although the GWR liked to imply (in its own publicity material) that 'road motors' were its own idea, this was not in fact true, and as mentioned above both the B&NCR and L&BR had experimented with motorized road feeder services. Nevertheless, the routes from Helston to the Lizard soon achieved particular importance; in part this was a reflection of the geographical situation of Helston station *vis-a-vis* outlying settlements such as Cadgwith and Lizard Town.

Ex-Lynton & Barnstaple Railway Milnes-Daimler 16 hp wagonette No. 1 leaving Helston for the Lizard on a demonstration run on 15th August, 1903, prior to the public service which started on 17th August. This vehicle was later allocated registration No. AF 37.   *Philip J. Kelley Collection*

Milnes-Daimler 16 hp wagonette Nos. 1 (*right*) and 2 (*left*) at the Lizard on 15th August, 1903. No. 2 was later allocated registration No. AF 36.   *Philip J. Kelley Collection*

No. 1 leaving Helston on 17th August, 1903, the first day of the public service to the Lizard.
Philip J. Kelley Collection

No. 2 poses outside the station at Helston; this ex-Lynton & Barnstaple Railway vehicle was entered from the rear and could carry 22 passengers. *Lens of Sutton Collection*

From 17th August to 17th October, 1903 both the open cars were run, but from 19th October one luggage motor omnibus seating 18 passengers and carrying luggage and parcels was substituted for the winter traffic. This photographic shows No. 1 as converted to an enclosed vehicle. The vehicle's livery appears to be varnished wood. *Philip J. Kelley Collection*

Twenty horse-power Milnes-Daimler No. 15 (AF 84, *left*) entered service on 18th May, 1904. To the right is 16 hp Milnes-Daimler No. 7 (AF 66) which entered service on 19th February of that year. A Milnes-Daimler private car (AF 18) is in the centre as these vehicles pose outside Hill's Hotel at the Lizard *circa* 1904. *Philip J. Kelley Collection*

GREAT WESTERN RAILWAY.

Motor Car and Omnibus Services.

Altered Service for Passengers, Mails and Luggage,
BETWEEN

HELSTON, MULLION, and THE LIZARD,

New Afternoon Trip: Lizard to Mullion & back,
Commencing on MONDAY, JULY 18th, 1904.

MOTOR OMNIBUSES, with accommodation for Luggage, and MOTOR CARS will run (condition of road permitting) as under, WEEK DAYS ONLY:—

TO MULLION AND THE LIZARD.

		p.m.	night.	a.m.	a.m.
London (Paddington)	dep.	9.50	12‖0	10.10	10.50
		a.m.	a.m.		p.m.
Bristol (Temple Meads)	,,	1. 7	3‖15	10.20	1. 0
Plymouth	,,	4 F 40	7 E 15	2 F 45	3 F 55
Newquay	,,	—	7.15	12.55	—
Falmouth	,,	—	9. 5	3.40	5.30
Truro	,,	6.30	9.45	4.1‖1	5.55
Redruth	,,	6.50	10.11	3 M 45	6.16
Camborne	,,	6.59	10.22	4 M 35	6.25
Penzance	,,	—	10.25	2. 0	4 D 40
St. Ives	,,	—	10.20	1.50	4 D 35
Hayle	,,	—	10.45	4 M 15	5 D 1
Helston Station	arr.	7.35	11.30	5 N 18	7.11

		Mail Car H	Motor Car	Luggage Omnibus	Motor Car	Motor Car	Lug. Bus.
		a.m.	a.m.	a.m.	p.m.	p.m.	p.m.
HELSTON STATION	dep.	7.45	11.35	11.40	—	5.20	7.15
DODSON'S GAP (for G'nwallo')	,,	—	—	—	—	—	—
CURY CROSS LANES (for Cury)	dep.	8.25	12.0	12.10	—	5.45	7.40
PENHALE (for Mullion)	,,	—	—	—	—	—	—
MULLION	,,	—	—	12.40	3.10	—	8.10
RUAN CROSS ROADS (for Cadgwith)	,,	—	—	—	—	—	—
HOUSEL ROAD	arr.	9. 5	12.43	1.13	3.53	6.28	8.43
THE LIZARD	,,	9. 0	12.45	1.15	3.55	6.30	8.45

FROM MULLION AND THE LIZARD.

		Motor Car	Luggage Omnibus	Motor Car	Luggage Omnibus	Mail Car H	Motor Car
		a.m.	a.m.	p.m.	p.m.	p.m.	p.m.
THE LIZARD	dep.	8.30	10. 0	2.15	3. 0	4.15	5. 0
HOUSEL ROAD	,,	8.32	10. 2	2.17	3. 2	—	5. 2
RUAN CROSS ROADS (for Cadgwith)	,,	—	—	—	—	—	—
PENHALE (for Mullion)	,,	—	—	2.45	—	—	—
MULLION	{ Arr. Dep. }	—	10.35	—	3 A 10	—	—
CURY CROSS LANES (for Cury)	,,	9. 0	10.50	—	3.40	4.40	5.30
DODSON'S GAP (for G'nwallo')	,,	—	—	—	—	—	—
HELSTON (Station)	arr.	9.40	11.30	—	4.10	5.30	6.10

		a.m.	a.m.	p.m.	p.m.	p.m.	p.m.
Helston (Station)	dep.	9 N 30	10.20	11.55	4.15	5.35	6 N 20 / 7 N 38
Hayle	arr.	10.37	—	12.40	5.21	6.39	9.15
St. Ives	,,	—	—	1. 0	—	—	—
Penzance	,,	10.55	—	1. 0	5.10	7.0	8.30
Camborne	,,	—	11 6	12.42	5.23	—	7. 5
Redruth	,,	—	11.17	12.55	5.30	—	7.14
Truro	,,	10.33	—	1.20	5.56	—	7.37
Falmouth	,,	—	—	12.25	1.55	6.30	8.12
Newquay	,,	—	—	1.55	5.30	8.43	10 S 50
Plymouth	,,	12 F 28	—	3 F 40	—	8 F 11	10 E 5
Bristol (Temple Meads)	,,	3.57	—	7.16	—	12.10	3 C 32
London (Paddington)	,,	5. 0	—	10.10	—	3.30	6 C 40
							a.m.

A.—Change at Penhale into 2.0 p.m. 'Bus from The Lizard.   C—Saturday nights and Sunday mornings excepted between Plymouth and London.
D—Passengers from Penzance, St. Ives, and Hayle by 4.40 p.m. train arrive Helston 5.45 p.m.   E—Millbay.   F—North Road.   G—Sunday mornings excepted.
M—Rail Motor Car: one class only.   N—Rail Motor Car Helston Branch: one class only.   S—Saturdays only.   ‡—Monday mornings excepted.

The Cars and Omnibuses will call (if required) at the intermediate places shewn. Passengers may also join at any other point on payment of fare from previous stage.

SINGLE JOURNEY FARES:—

Between HELSTON and	Lug. Motor Car	Between DODSON'S GAP and	Lug. Motor Car	Between CURY CROSS LANES and	Lug. Motor Car	Between PENHALE and	Lug. Motor Car	Between MULLION and	Lug. Motor Car	Between RUAN CROSS ROADS and	Lug. Motor Car	Between THE LIZARD and	Lug. Motor Car	Between MULLION and	Lug. Motor Car
Dodson's Gap	3d. 6d.	Helston Station	3d. 6d.	Dodson's Gap	3d. 6d.	Helston Station	6d. 9d.	The Lizard	6d. 9d.	Ruan Cross		Ruan Cross			
Cury Cross Lanes	6d. 9d.	Cury Cross Lanes	3d. 6d.	Helston Station	6d. 9d.	Cury Cross	3d. 6d.	Penhale	3d. 6d.	Roads	3d. 6d.	Roads	3d. 6d.	The Lizard	6d. 9d.
Penhale	9d. 1/-	Penhale	6d. 9d.	Penhale	3d. 6d.	Mullion	3d.	Mullion	6d.	Mullion	6d.	Penhale	6d.	Penhale	3d.
Mullion	1/-	Mullion	9d.	Mullion	3d. 6d.	Dodson's Gap	6d. 9d.	Cury Cross	6d.	Cury Cross		Cury Cross		Cury Cross	
Ruan Cross Roads	1/- 1.3	Ruan Cross Roads	9d. 1/-	Ruan Cross Roads	6d. 9d.	Ruan Cross Roads	3d. 6d.	Dodson's Gap	9d. 1/-	Dodson's Gap	1/- 1.3	Lanes	9d. 1/-	Lanes	6d.
The Lizard	1/- 1.6	The Lizard	1/- 1.3	The Lizard	9d. 1/-	The Lizard	6d. 9d.	Helston	1/- 1.3	Helston		Dodson's Gap	1/- 1.3	Dodson's Gap	9d.
												Helston	1/- 1/6	Helston	1/-

H.—Motor Car fares will be charged by the MAIL CAR.
TIME TABLES.—The Directors give notice that the Company do not undertake that the Cars or Omnibuses shall start or arrive at the times specified in the Bills; nor will they be accountable for any loss, inconvenience, or injury which may arise from delay or detention.
Tickets will be issued on the Car or Omnibus and must be retained until completion of journey.

Through Railway Tickets will not be issued on, nor by, these Motor Cars or Omnibuses.

Booking Seats.—Passengers may book seats on the Motor Cars or Omnibuses at the Railway Stations, and at the Company's Receiving Office at The Lizard (Hill's) Hotel, or the through journey between Helston and The Lizard.

Passengers' Luggage.—Hand Luggage will be carried free.
Heavy or bulky Luggage which can be conveyed by the Cars or Omnibuses without inconvenience to passengers will be charged for at the rate of 4d. to 6d. per package, according to size and weight.

Luggage in Advance.—Luggage sent in advance of passengers will be conveyed between the Railway Station at Helston and the Company's Receiving Office at The Lizard (Hill's) Hotel, and at Messrs. George & Son's, Mullion, at a charge of 1d. per package.

Bicycles.—Bicycles will be carried, when they can be conveyed without inconvenience to passengers, at a charge of 1/- each.

Parcels and Light Goods Traffic. Light Goods and Parcels will be conveyed by the Omnibuses between Helston Station, Cury Cross Lanes, Mullion, and The Lizard, at the following charges:—Packages up to 7-lbs., 3d.; 8 lbs. to 28 lbs., 4d.; 29 lbs. to 56 lbs., 6d.; 57 lbs. to 112 lbs., 9d. These may be handed in at the Railway Station at Helston, at the Receiving Office at The Lizard (Hill's) Hotel, at Messrs. George & Son's, Mullion, and at the Wheel Inn, Cury Cross Lanes, or to the Conductor en route.

For Parcels conveyed between The Lizard and Mullion, The Lizard and Cury Cross Lanes, a minimum charge of 3d. will be made.

Paddington,
July 4th, 1904.

JAMES C. INGLIS.
General Manager.

Timetable of the Helston, Mullion and Lizard service dated 4th July, 1904.

Philip J. Kelley Collection

Milnes-Daimler 16 hp composite single-deck omnibus No. 8 is seen at Helston station in 1904. Note the acetylene lamp on the front of the roof. This vehicle entered service on 31st March, 1904 for goods, mail and passengers (10 inside and two beside the driver). The goods compartment could also be used by passengers by means of flap seats and no smoking was allowed in the compartment. *Philip J. Kelley Collection*

No. 8 (registration No. A 4260) poses for the photographer at Bochym Hill near Mullion, between the Lizard and Helston in 1904. *Philip J. Kelley Collection*

THE LINE IN OPERATION

The Lizard peninsula was more of an isthmus than a peninsula, as it had the sea to the west, south and east, and the Helford River to the north. Access to this remote region was via a narrow neck of land with Helston conveniently-sited at its centre, and with no rival railways in the vicinity, Helston station naturally became a focus for carrier services from outlying parts. Thus, at the end of the 19th century, St Keverne was linked to the station by Mr Tipconey's horse bus; journey time, for the 12 mile journey, was up to two hours (and travellers were expected to walk up steep hills to help the horse!). The new motor buses supplemented these existing local services, and in time largely superseded them.

Sadly, the first few months of motor bus operation were marred by an explosion and fire in the road motor shed at Helston on 29th September, 1904. This incident, in which one driver was injured, resulted in the destruction of two vehicles as described in *The Times* on 1st October, 1904:

> Fire broke out on Thursday night in the motor car shed at Helston railway station, Cornwall, and caused the destruction of two cars belonging to the Great Western Railway Company. One of these was used for mail traffic in the district, and the other, a nearly new Jersey car, for passengers. When the fire broke out, about half past nine o'clock, a man named Bailey was lying under the mail car doing some repairs, and another driver named Sanders was about other work in the shed. Sanders dragged Bailey from under the car, and both had to make a dash for the door. Bailey was badly burnt on the right hand and arm, and less severely on the leg. The two cars ignited in an incredibly short time, and the building, which was of wood and corrugated iron, was soon unapproachable. The petrol tank of the Jersey car exploded with a report like that of a cannon and, tearing a hole in the side of the shed, went up like a gigantic rocket, alighting finally in a field 300 or 400 yards away. There were several minor explosions.

As a result of this unfortunate incident, the road motor service was suspended between October 1904 and April 1905. Ironically, the GWR had already announced that the buses would be withdrawn, following a dispute with the local authority over the very poor state of the roads - which the council refused to repair as no steam roller was available. In the event, both buses were subsequently rebuilt, and one of the re-bodied vehicles (No. 8) was later returned to service on the Lizard route. Meanwhile, the condition of the local roads had been much improved after the Great Western had loaned one of its own steam rollers to Cornwall County Council.

The early buses clanked, snorted and 'smeeched' their way to the Lizard; they tore up the roads with their solid tyres and frequently broke down, but they had come to stay. It was the beginning of a new era, and within the next 20 years regular services were operating daily to most of the villages in the Meneage area, and the 'splendid old horse buses', so familiar a feature of town and village life, went out of service. In the early days the Lizard bus, in addition to the conveyance of passengers, parcels and luggage, carried the Royal Mail for Ruan Minor - the bus being met at Ruan crossroads by a postman with a donkey and cart, so that the mail could be conveniently transferred.

A second bus service was introduced on 10th October, 1909, this time between Helston and Porthleven. After World War I this was followed by a rapid expansion of GWR motor bus services, and within a few years regular

Dennis 20 hp single-deck omnibus No. 159. This vehicle entered traffic on 3rd August, 1911. No. 159 is seen at Ruan Cross Roads which appears to be a general interchange between the GWR buses and a local horse bus.
Philip J. Kelley Collection

From 1st May, 1904 the General Post Office entered in to a contract with the GWR 'Road Motors' to carry mails between Helston and the Lizard. This photograph, taken about 1912, shows Dennis single-deck omnibus No. 159 at Ruan Cross Roads exchanging mails with the local postman and his donkey cart.
Philip J. Kelley Collection

THE LINE IN OPERATION

local services were operating from Helston to Mullion, St Keverne, Coverack, Porthallow, Porthoustock, Manaccan, Gunwalloe, Redruth and Camborne. There was also a useful through service from Falmouth to Penzance via Penryn, Mabe, Longdowns, Helston, Porthleven, Breage, Ashton and Marazion.

In the course of time, individual operators who had introduced private services were taken over by the larger companies until only two main operators remained in the Helston area, namely, the Great Western Railway and the Cornwall Motor Transport Co. Having established themselves, the operators soon realised that the road and rail interests were complementary rather than competitive, and that co-operation was necessary if further wasteful competition was to be eliminated.

The buses used on the routes to and from Helston station were of varied design and appearance. Many had Milnes-Daimler chassis, but bodywork and seating arrangements were noticeably varied - some vehicles having open, or semi-open bodies while others were fully enclosed. Nos. 1 and 2 - the former Lynton & Barnstaple buses - originally had semi-open bodies with virtually flat roofs and no window glass; passengers entered the vehicles via rear exits. At a later date, car No. 1 (and probably also No. 2) received a fairly substantial wooden body with two large windows on either side.

Another bus used on the original Helston-Lizard route was car No. 3 which, like its ex-L&BR companions, was a 16 hp Milnes-Daimler vehicle with accommodation for about 22 travellers. Car No. 4 was substantially similar, although this bus - delivered in time for the 1905 winter service - was a 20 hp vehicle. Further motor buses arrived from the manufacturers at intervals throughout 1904-05, cars 8 and 9 - both 20 hp Milnes-Daimlers - being among those used on the Helston services. As we have seen, car No. 8 had the misfortune to be incinerated in the fire at Helston in September 1905 but, despite the total destruction of all non-metal parts, it was given a new wooden body and returned to service in 1905 (the other severely-damaged vehicle - No. 3 - was rebuilt as a lorry).

Car N. 8 was fitted-up as a 'luggage omnibus', for which purpose it was equipped with a luggage compartment in addition to the main passenger saloon. Under normal circumstances, the luggage compartment could carry up to a ton of parcels or passengers' luggage, although it could also, when necessary, be used as a passenger compartment. In May 1904 a contemporary press account revealed that, on one occasion, a GWR 'luggage omnibus' had carried 'a record number of passengers' between Lizard Town and Helston, twelve passengers being accommodated in the saloon, while seven more were somehow squeezed into the luggage space, two were seated alongside the driver, and three fearless travellers managed to find a place among the luggage on the roof!

A summary of some of the earliest buses used on the Lizard route is given in *Table One*. These vehicles were in service during the Edwardian era, the numbers given being a sample collation rather than a complete list of every GWR bus or charabanc used between Helston and the Lizard prior to World War I.

Mail changing taking place at Cross Lanes post office. The vehicle is Wolseley 33 hp omnibus No. 88 (AF 268) which entered service on 5th June, 1907. *Philip J. Kelley Collection*

Most of the road motor halts in the Lizard Peninsula were merely roadside stopping places, but at Coverack local residents helped to finance the erection of a proper waiting shelter.
Philip J. Kelley Collection

THE LINE IN OPERATION

Table One

GWR motor buses used on the Helston routes circa 1903-1914

GWR No.	Reg. No.	Type	Notes
1	AF37	Milnes-Daimler 16 hp	Ex L&BR vehicle
2	AF36	Milnes-Daimler 16 hp	Ex-L&BR vehicle
3	AF38	Milnes-Daimler 16 hp	Rebuilt as lorry after fire
4	AF61	Milnes-Daimler 20 hp	
8	A4260	Milnes-Daimler 20 hp	Rebodied after fire
9	A5014	Milnes-Daimler 20 hp	
13	BH09	Milnes-Daimler 20 hp	
20	A6181	Milnes-Daimler 20 hp	
156	T2100	Dennis 20 hp	
159	AF718	Dennis 20 hp	

The buses were usually painted in a variant of the Great Western coaching stock livery, though photographic evidence shows that some examples were painted in an overall brown or 'varnished wood' colour scheme (the standard Milnes-Daimler livery was brown, and this may, at least partly, explain the appearance of plain brown-liveried motor buses during the early 1900s).

Photographs, now in the National Railway Museum, reveal several livery variations, even among buses adorned in the 'standard' chocolate and cream livery. Car No. 9, for example, was at one time painted in a lined cream livery with a broad chocolate band at waist height, the bonnet, chassis, lower body panels and upper body being cream, while the GWR coat of arms was displayed on the brown part of the bodywork. A similar photograph shows that car No. 20 was similarly adorned, but in this case the bonnet and chassis appear to have been painted chocolate-brown; this same livery was carried by car No. 8 after its rebuilding in 1904. An overall brown livery was in use during World War I, and some vehicles also appeared in a short-lived green colour scheme.

Other types of vehicle were employed on the Lizard services after World War I, when Dennis, Thornycroft and Burford vehicles were introduced on the Helston routes. Car No. 567, for instance, was a solid-tyred Burford single deck bus dating from 1923; its passenger saloon was fully glazed but the driver still sat in an open-fronted cab. Car No. 352 - a 1924 Chevrolet - was, however, of more modern design, with an enclosed cab and pneumatic tyres. Details of some of the varied vehicles employed in the Lizard area in the 1920s appear in *Table Two*.

Table Two

Some GWR motor buses used on the Helston routes circa 1920-1928

GWR No.	Reg. No.	Type	Notes
197	T6674	AEC 45 hp charabanc	
352	XU2159	Chevrolet 22 hp	
567	XO6588	Burford	Scrapped 1932
939	YK3833	Thornycroft A1	Sold 1931

An unidentified 'Metro' class 2-4-0T enters Helston staion in 1933. The engine shed siding can be seen to the left.
R.W. Kidner

A 'Metro' class pauses during a break in shunting duties at Helston in August 1933.
R.W. Kidner

The Helston motor bus services were probably at their peak during the 1920s, by which time a multiplicity of routes had been introduced - not only to destinations in the Lizard peninsula but also to places to the north of Helston, such as Penzance, Redruth and Falmouth. Some of these services actually competed with the railway, while the ease with which Sunday bus services could be arranged gave the Great Western operating authorities little incentive to run Sunday train services between Helston and Gwinear Road. The element of competition between road and rail transport could easily be contained so long as the Helston bus services remained in GWR hands, but in the longer term the railway probably aided its competitors by establishing so many useful motor bus routes in the Lizard area.

The GWR was, by this time, one of the largest bus operators in the country, and it seemed that the company would continue to expand and develop its huge road motor fleet as an important adjunct to the rail network. Unfortunately, the undoubted success of the Great Western bus fleet led to complaints from the road transport industry to the effect that the GWR (and other railway companies) did not have Parliamentary consent to operate road services, and for this reason the railway bus routes were said to be illegal. There was an element of truth in the allegation of illegality, and to formalize the situation whereby the GWR could operate its road services the company obtained new Powers under the provisions of the Great Western (Road Transport) Act 1928. This new legislation enabled the GWR to own, work and use motor vehicles in its own right, and to enter into arrangements with other parties for the operation of road transport services.

By virtue these Powers, the Great Western Railway acquired a substantial financial interest in the National Omnibus & Transport Company, and all GWR motor buses in an area bounded by Penzance and Moretonhampstead were transferred to that undertaking on the understanding that the bus company would not compete with the railway. This agreement - which was arrived at after much negotiation - was supposed to lead to greater co-ordination between road and rail transport; it nevertheless signalled the end of the GWR road motor services. The Helston services were relinquished on and from 1st January, 1929 and, by the end of 1933, all of the Great Western motor bus services had been taken over by the newly-created Western National Omnibus Company, or other 'railway associated' bus companies.

Trains and Traffic in the 1930s

There were, by the 1930s, still around nine passenger trains each way, with additional workings on summer Saturdays. The July 1935 working timetable provides a useful glimpse of the Helston branch in operation at the height of its popularity as a summer holiday line. The basic weekday service comprised nine up and nine down workings. In the up direction, northbound up workings left Helston at 6.35, 7.50, 9.50 am, 12.10, 1.40, 4.00, 5.35, 7.05 and 8.35 pm - the 6.35 am and 5.35 pm services being 'mixed' workings that conveyed both passenger and goods vehicles. In the reverse direction, down workings departed from

HELSTON BRANCH.

Single Line worked by Electric Train Staff between Helston and Gwinear Road. Crossing Places, Helston, Nancegollan Loop and Gwinear Road.

Week Days only.

Distance from Gwinear Rd. and M.P. Mileage.	Station No.	STATIONS.	Ruling gradient 1 in	Time allowance for Ordinary Freight Trains. See page 2.		Passenger. dep. A.M.	Passenger. dep. A.M.	Goods. arr. A.M.	Goods. dep. A.M.	Mixed. arr. A.M.	Mixed. dep. A.M.	Passenger. arr. P.M.	Passenger. dep. P.M.	Passenger. arr. P.M.	Passenger. dep. P.M.	Passenger. § SO arr. P.M.	Passenger. § SO dep. P.M.	Passenger. ¶ arr. P.M.	Passenger. ¶ dep. P.M.	Passenger. arr. P.M.	Passenger. dep. P.M.	Passenger. dep. P.M.	Mixed. dep. P.M.	Empty. ‡ dep. P.M.
				Point to point times. Mins.	Allow for stop. Mins.	Allow for start. Mins.																			
—	2085	Gwinear Road	60 R	—	—	—	7 10	—	—	9 17	—	10 50	—	1 5	2 47	2 35	—	4 22	—	6 15	7 40	9 35	10 40
1	2281	Praze	67 F	8	1	1	7 18	CS	9 42	CS	10 58	CS	1 13	2 50	2 43	—	4 30	4 58	6 23	7 48	9 43	CS
3	2282	Stop Board	60 F	—	—	—	—	—	9 27	9 58	P	—	—	—	2 49	—	—	—	—	—	—	—
4	2283	Nancegollan	61 R	6	1	1	CS	CS	9 48	P 9 50	CS	CS	1 19	2 60	2 52	CS	4 39	CS	CS	CS	CS	CS
7	2284	Truthall Platform	61 R	—	—	—	7 21	9 6	9 53	10 5	11 4	—	1 24	—	2 59	—	—	5 4	6 29	7 54	9 49	—
8	2285	Helston Stop Board	—	—	—	—	—	9 12	10 8	10 38	—	P	—	—	—	—	—	—	—	—	8 0	9 55	—
8 67	2285	Helston	61 R	10	1	1	7 32	9 17	10 50	—	11 15	—	1 30	3 3	—	—	4 46	—	—	6 40	8 5	10 0	11 5

Distance.	Station No.	STATIONS.	Ruling gradient 1 in	Point to point times. Mins.	Allow for stop. Mins.	Allow for start. Mins.	Mixed. arr. A.M.	Mixed. dep. A.M.	Passenger. arr. A.M.	Passenger. dep. A.M.	Passenger. arr. A.M.	Passenger. dep. A.M.	Passenger. arr. P.M.	Passenger. dep. P.M.	Goods. arr. P.M.	Goods. dep. P.M.	Passenger. SO dep. P.M.	Passenger. SX dep. P.M.	Passenger. arr. P.M.	Passenger. dep. P.M.	Passenger. dep. P.M.	Passenger. dep. P.M.
M. C.																						
—	1 67	Helston	61 R	—	—	—	—	6 35	7 50	—	9 50	12 10	1 20	—	—	2 45	3 45	4 0	5 35	—	7 12	8 35	10 10
1 58	2 67	Truthall Platform	66 K	1	—	—	—	—	7 57	8 4	12 17	12 21	CS	1 52	2 17	XC 2 48	3 52	4 7	5 42	CS	7 19	8 42	CS
3 45	3 58	Nancegollan	60 R	10	1	1	—	6 46	CS	CS	10 5	CS	CS	1 58	2 53	P 3 3	CS	4 11	5 49	5 55	7 25	8 49	CS
5 79	4 6	Nancegollan Loop	60 R	6	—	—	—	—	8 10	—	10 7	12 25	—	—	3 16	P 3 18	—	4 20	CS	—	—	CS	CS
7 67	5 7	Praze	61 F	6	1	—	—	6 52	8 17	—	10 14	12 31	2 5	—	3 24	—	4 12	4 27	—	6 2	7 32	9 2	10 26
8 67	6 8	Gwinear Rd. Stop Board	61 F	2	—	—																		
	6 8	Gwinear Road					6 59		8 17		10 14 12 37													

‡ Runs only on August Bank Holiday, Monday, August 5th. § Will not run after September 14th. ¶ Depart 4.55 p.m. on Saturdays and run 5 minutes later throughout.

Great Western Railway working timetable for July 1935.

Gwinear Road at 7.10, 8.52, 10.50 am, 1.05, 2.35, 4.50, 6.15, 7.4 and 9.35 pm. The 10.50 am and 9.35 pm services were 'mixed' workings, while goods traffic was also conveyed by a daily pick-up service that left Gwinear Road at 9.17 am and returned from Helston at 2.05 pm. The normal journey time was 25 minutes in each direction.

An additional train ran on Saturday, the up service leaving Helston at 3.45 pm, while the balancing down working was scheduled to depart from Gwinear Road at 4.22 pm. Although there were no advertised through workings to or from London, the GWR provided a special, non-stop evening train on Monday 5th August (Bank Holiday Monday) that was scheduled to leave Helston at 10.10 pm and reach Gwinear Road in the creditable time of 18 minutes. Travellers on this service were able to travel through to Paddington by means of a sleeping car train from Penzance.

The summer 1939 timetable was slightly better than its 1935 predecessor, in that there were 10 trains each way on ordinary weekdays, with an extra working on summer Saturdays. The special Bank Holiday evening service was provided on 7th and 8th August, enabling through travellers to reach Gwinear Road in 17 minutes, in time to connect with a special 10.10 pm sleeping car service from Penzance that arrived in Paddington by 6.35 am on the following morning.

Most services were worked by '45XX' or '55XX' class 'Small Prairies', and the usual formation was one of the familiar Great Western two-coach 'B sets'; many services conveyed 'siphons' at the rear. Goods traffic was of considerable importance, and in addition to the usual staples of coal inwards and agricultural produce outwards the branch carried large amounts of perishables such as flowers and broccoli. Broccoli, in fact, was an important source of freight traffic on the Helston line, and in 1936 no less than 30,000 tons were sent from Helston and other stations in West Cornwall. Broccoli consignments were usually dispatched in standard Great Western 'Mex' cattle wagons; long rakes of these vehicles could often be seen in the sidings at Helston or Gwinear Road, while in times of particularly heavy traffic ordinary open wagons were also pressed into service.

Quarry traffic was also of great importance, and the line served various granite and other workings around the Lizard area. There was at one time a special quarry siding at the terminus, but this was lifted during the 1930s depression; in 1956, however, it was re-laid in connection with an upsurge of serpentine rock traffic, special loading chutes being provided to facilitate the rapid transfer of stone from road to rail vehicles.

The freight vehicles used on the Gwinear Road to Helston line reflected the types of traffic carried, and in addition to the 'Mex' wagons mentioned above there were large numbers of ordinary opens for coal or general merchandise traffic. Meat traffic was conveyed in 'Micas' or white-painted 'Mica B' vans, while general merchandise traffic was typically carried in ordinary Great Western 'Mink' covered vans. As usual on Great Western lines, the branch had its own 'Toad' brake van, this vehicle being restricted to use between Gwinear Road and Helston; in recognition of this fact, it carried the legend 'Helston RU' on its sides.

The Helston gas works, an important local customer is said to have acquired a small fleet of privately-owned coal wagons for its own use, these vehicle being painted black with the owner's name in block letters. A sketch of 12-ton seven-plank wagon No. 10 lettered 'Helston Gas Co', was shown in the June 1969 *Model Railway News*, illustrating an article by Peter Matthews. Wagon Nos. 10, 20, 30 and 40 were said to have been 'built in 1926 by D.G. Hall & Co. Ltd of Swansea and registered by the GWR', but this raises a problem, insofar as the Helston Gas Light Co. had been acquired by Helston Corporation in 1924, and in 1934, the corporation sold the business to the newly-registered Helston & District Gas Company. No wagons were registered by the GWR in the names of either Helston Corporation or the Helston Gas Light Company, though it is possible that wagons could have been on hire. D.G. Hall & Co.'s works at Newport began building wagons in 1938, but there are no details of this undertaking having a works at Swansea. In 1937, the Gloucester Railway Carriage & Wagon Co. hired three 12-ton wagons to the gas company for a period of three years, followed by a fourth in 1938, also for three years.

Apart from the passenger traffic, there were periods of great activity on Flora Day in connection with the Horse Show, many horse boxes being dealt with. The much larger Royal Cornwall Show was held at Helston on several occasions - Helston being the centre of a very large agricultural district. In addition to horses and other livestock, there was a heavy traffic in agricultural implements, farm machinery, and other show exhibits. Inwards traffic began to flow about three weeks before the show date and built-up to a peak about four or five days before the opening day. Extra staff and cartage equipment were drafted to the town to deal with this traffic, and it was a point of honour that everything on hand should be delivered before the opening time. There was always the closest co-operation between the show and the railway officials, which resulted in general satisfaction being expressed at the effort made.

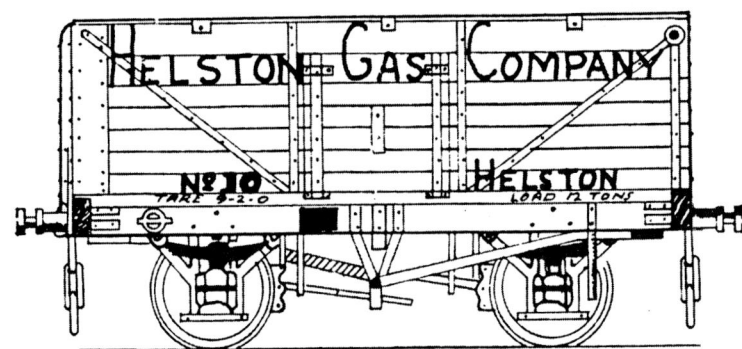

A conjectural impression of 'Helston Gas Company' 12-ton open wagon No. 10. No such wagon was registered with the GWR, although it is conceivable that the vehicle was on hire.

Rural Collection & Delivery Services

In the same way as the coming of the steam age and of the railway brought great changes in the life of the nation, so the development of the motor car created a revolution of tremendous importance. The change was very gradual at first and made little impact, but road transport gained considerable momentum after World War I, when surplus army vehicles were obtainable at very low prices, and were used to an ever increasing extent in the development of bus and road haulage undertakings.

Competition became exceptionally keen, especially where vulnerable freight traffic was concerned. The railways were hampered by reason of their common carrier obligations, whereas the road haulage concerns had freedom of choice, and largely freedom of movement, until some restrictions were imposed by the licensing authority. Up to this time, the collection and delivery of general merchandise within the 'free cartage area' at Helston (which, generally speaking was the area within the town boundary) was performed by horse-drawn vans. In the early 1920s the horses were dispensed with and the town cartage service was handed over to an agent, who introduced motor transport. There were also other agents, one at Porthleven and the other at Mullion, who collected and delivered traffic once or twice weekly, or as required, in their respective areas. In addition, many horse-drawn buses from the villages in the Meneage area called at the station on Mondays and Saturdays to collect goods and parcels for the outlying places.

The Great Western Railway Company, a pioneer of passenger road transport and many other ancillary services, was not slow to realise the implications and advantages of road transport for the collection and delivery of freight traffic. About the year 1925, they introduced a country lorry service at Helston, primarily for the daily collection of dairy produce from two dairy firms in the district. This service was so satisfactory and so much appreciated that other traders were soon asking for similar services, and it was not long before the country lorry service was expanded to cover the whole of the Lizard peninsula, the Meneage district and the Porthleven and Breage area. The town agency was taken over shortly after by the Great Western, as were the agencies at Porthleven and Mullion.

By 1938, Helston station had emerged as an important railhead for the Lizard area, with locally-based road vehicles providing extensive feeder services to villages such as Porthallow (12 miles), Kynance Cove (12 miles) and Porthoustock (12 miles). It should, perhaps, be pointed out that most Great Western rural stations served comparatively small catchment areas that extended for perhaps five miles on each side of the railway - Blenheim & Woodstock, for instance, served nowhere more than four miles from the station, while Faringdon-based road vehicles operated no further than six miles from the railway. Helston, in contrast, served an area extending south and eastwards for over 12 miles.

An idea of the large size of Helston's rural hinterland can be obtained by an examination of an 896-page GWR staff publication entitled *Towns, Villages & Outlying Works Etc. Served by the Great Western Railway*, which was published in

Table Three
Goods and Parcels delivery arrangements at Helston, 1938

Name of place	Distance from Helston	Delivery arrangements
Ashton	5 miles	Lorry service
Bochym	5 miles	Lorry service
Bosaham	10 miles	Lorry service
Breage	3½ miles	Lorry service
Cadgwith	12 miles	Lorry service
Carleen*	5 miles	Lorry or Western National bus
Church Town (Lizard)	11 miles	Lorry service
Chynhale*	3 miles	Lorry service
Chyvarloe	3 miles	Lorry service
Cornwall Mines (Breage)	5 miles	Lorry service
Constantine*	7 miles	Lorry, carrier, or Western National
Coverack	11 miles	Lorry service
Cury	5 miles	Lorry service
Dean Coverack Quarries	11 miles	Lorry service
Germoe	7 miles	Lorry service
Grade	10 miles	Lorry service
Godolphin Cross	5 miles	Lorry service
Gunwalloe	6 miles	Lorry service
Gweek Wharf	4 miles	Lorry service
Gweek	4 miles	Lorry service
Halabezak	6 miles	Lorry service
Helston	n/a	Free cartage area
Helford	10 miles	Lorry service
Kynance Cove	12 miles	Lorry service
Laity	4 miles	Lorry service
Lanarth	12 miles	Lorry service
Landewednack	11 miles	Lorry service
Lizard, The	11 miles	Lorry service
Lowertown	2 miles	Lorry service
Manaccan	11 miles	Lorry service
Mawgan-in-Meneage	4 miles	Lorry service
Mullion	8 miles	Lorry service
Newtown (Germoe)	6 miles	Lorry service
Pengerzick	6 miles	Lorry service
Penrose	2½ miles	Lorry service
Poldhu	7½ miles	Lorry service
Polpeer	12 miles	Lorry service
Porthallow	12 miles	Lorry service
Prospidnick*	4 miles	Lorry service
Porthleven	4 miles	Lorry service
Porthoustock	12 miles	Lorry service
Praa Sands	7 miles	Lorry service
Praa Syndicate Works	6 miles	Lorry service
Predannack Woolas	9 miles	Lorry service
Ruan Major	10 miles	Lorry service
Ruan Minor	11 miles	Lorry service
St Anthony-in-Meneage	12 miles	Lorry service
St Breage	3½ miles	Lorry service
St Keverne	11 miles	Lorry service
St Keverne Stone Quarrie	12 miles	Lorry service
St Martin-in-Meneage	12 miles	Lorry service
Sithney	3 miles	Lorry service
Trelowarren	5 miles	Lorry service
Trenear	3 miles	Lorry service
Trescowe	7 miles	Lorry service
Trewennack	1¾ miles	Lorry service
Wendron	2 miles	Lorry service

* Also served from Nancegollan or other local stations.

1938 as an 'at a glance' guide to the collection and delivery arrangements for goods and parcels at each station throughout the Great Western system. This large green volume listed all places served by the company, together with the mode of conveyance from the nearest GWR station. Some sample information from the book of *Towns, Villages & Outlying Works* is given in *Table Three*, which provides a useful insight into the way in which the Great Western Railway provided a door-to-door service during the later 1930s. The table shows various villages and hamlets in the Helston area, the name of each location being listed on the extreme left. The delivery arrangements for each village are shown to the right, together with the approximate distance from Helston station.

To put this information into perspective one might also consider *Table Four*, which compares the size of Helston's service area with those of two comparable Great Western branch line stations. It will be seen that, in terms of both size and complexity, the network of rural delivery services radiating from Helston was much bigger than usual.

Table Four

The service areas of Helston and other GWR stations

Station	Villages served	Maximum distance of delivery service
Helston	50+	12 miles
Bourton-on-the-Water	1	6 miles
Faringdon	20	6 miles
Blenheim & Woodstock	9	4 miles

The success of Helston's road delivery services led to the development of the cartage of non-railborne traffic, consisting mainly of the conveyance of road stone for county and local authorities, together with cement, sand and concrete blocks for builders and merchants, manures and feeding stuffs for farmers, and many other bulk loads.

For this class of work suitable equipment was supplied by the provision of an end and side tipping 5-ton lorry, as well as a 6-ton rigid lorry. There were also five 30 cwt or 2 ton vans for general cartage on the town and country routes, and three specially constructed lorries for dealing with milk traffic in churns; this involved the daily collection from farms in the area, conveyance by road to Lostwithiel, and the return of empty churns from the factory to the farms.

The road services of the railway were also used in the development of household removals. A railway container, of the 'B' or 'BX' type, loaded on the six-ton lorry was used for this purpose; packing and unpacking was performed by a local professional packer, who supplied his own packing materials. Charges were based upon a fixed hourly charge for the lorry and driver, calculated on the estimated time it would take to perform the whole operation, plus running costs on a mileage basis, wages of any additional labour employed, plus the packer's charge and a per-centage charge for profit and contingencies.

For longer distances the container would be brought to Helston station, transferred to a vacuum-fitted railway wagon and forwarded by fast freight train under the railways' 'Green Arrow' system of transport, which ensured that the consignment maintained the connecting services and reached its destination at the scheduled time. Previous arrangements had been made for the delivery, unloading and unpacking services, the charges for which were included in the 'all in' quotation. In course of time the GWR obtained an interest in Messrs Pickfords Ltd, who then took over all the removal services previously carried out by the railway.

The conditions outlined above continued up to the outbreak of World War II, with the railway doing all in its power to fight the ever increasing road competition by quoting competitive rates and making the fullest use of the rail and road services that they were able to offer.

Other Developments

In the mid-1920s the company carried out a thorough review of its entire branch line operations and, as a result, a programme of economies was put into effect. In a very few cases it was reluctantly agreed that closures would have to take place, but in general the GWR preferred to inroduce operating economies such as track rationalization or staff cuts. In the latter context, smaller stations such as Praze lost their station masters, the stations concerned being placed under the control of larger stations such as Nancegollan or Helston.

In another attempt to introduce more efficient methods of operation on the Gwinear Road to Helston line, the GWR introduced mechanized methods of line maintenance, with reduced numbers of permanent way men using permanent way trolleys for inspection and maintenance work. In earlier days, work of this kind had been carried out by gangers who patrolled their sections of line on foot, but the introduction of manual or petrol-driven permanent way vehicles enabled each permanent way gang to cover a much greater length of track.

To facilitate this mode of operation the Helston branch was fitted with a gangers' occupation key system, so that permanent way gangs could have complete possession of the single line sections upon which they were working. This system worked in conjunction with the normal single line signalling system, the idea being that, when an occupation key was withdrawn by the ganger, no trains could enter the section of line upon which work was taking place.

There were, in all, 10 occupation key huts between Gwinear Road and Helston, while other occupation key instruments were installed in signal cabins or other convenient locations. In general, the instruments were sited at intervals of a one mile or less, Hut No. 1, for example, being positioned at 1 mile 0 chains, just 75 chains to the south of Gwinear Road West signal box, while Hut No. 2 was sited a little over one mile further on at 2 mile 2 chains. Each occupation key hut was equipped with an occupation key instrument, and a telephone link to the signalman responsible for the section concerned.

A Line of Character

The Helston branch was a vital link between Helston and the outside world, but on a more intimate level it was also part of the local community. Station staff, train crews and habitual travellers were often close personal friends - indeed, in an isolated area such as west Cornwall many people were related to each other. The trains themselves were regarded as part of the landscape, the green engines and chocolate and cream coaches being a familiar sight throughout Cornwall and the western counties. This relationship between the GWR and the areas it served was carefully fostered by the company's public relations department, maps; posters, books, jig-saw puzzles and a wide range of promotional literature being used to bolster the Great Western's image as the 'Holiday Line'.

Curiously, the Helston branch sometimes appeared to be somewhat apart from the rest of the Great Western system. There existed a relationship between the townspeople and traders generally, and the railway staff, which probably stemmed from the early days when so many of the local people were promoters, Directors or shareholders of the Helston Railway Company.

In those early days, the GWR district offices were situated at Penzance, but it was not long before they were closed and Plymouth became the district centre. The head offices were of course at Paddington, but to one in the far south west, whether he was a Cornishman by birth or adoption, Plymouth was far away and Paddington very remote, not only in mileage and geographical position, but because of the fact that both of these distant places were situated somewhere up country 'in England'. This created a feeling of independence which, wisely, was not frowned upon by those in higher authority, and which was certainly not abused.

World War II

On 3rd September, 1939, a deteriorating international situation culminated in the outbreak of World War II, and with horrific memories of the 1914-1918 conflict still fresh in many people's minds, it was expected that Britain would soon be devastated by fleets of massed Nazi bombers. Happily, pre-war 'experts' had wildly exaggerated the destructive capabilities of the dreaded Luftwaffe, and the first months of war were so uneventful that people began to speak derisively of the 'Phoney War'.

For rail travellers, the nightly 'blackout' and the sight of soldiers, sailors and airmen in uniform were reminders that there was a 'war on', while holiday lines such as the Helston route no longer carried large numbers of summer holidaymakers. In the summer of 1940, the station nameboards at Helston and the intermediate stations were removed in an attempt to confuse Nazi parachutists and 'Fifth Columnists'!

Although the war resulted in a diminution in the numbers of holidaymakers travelling on the branch, petrol rationing and the restrictions placed on road traffic after the outbreak of war ensured that rail traffic - especially freight -

'44XX' class 2-6-2T No. 4408 stands alongside the platform at Helston with a down train.
P.Q. Treloar

A general view of Helston station *circa* 1930s, showing the rear of an up train alongside the single platform, with the goods shed visible to the right.
Lens of Sutton Collection

increased considerably, and the Helston line was soon playing a very full part in the war effort.

In the early days of World War II the branch brought scores of youthful 'evacuees' from London and other centres of population, and many of these city-bred boys and girls remained in the Helston area for the duration of the war. More importantly, the line also carried large numbers of servicemen to and from aerodromes or other military establishments on the Lizard peninsula.

The Lizard, area had traditionally been regarded as a strategically-important region, its geographical position *vis-à-vis* the Western Approaches being a prime consideration in time of war. In 1588, observation posts on the Lizard had given early warning of the Spanish Armada, while in World War I the Royal Naval Air Service had established an airship station at nearby Mullion. Similarly, in World War II, the Lizard was of great importance, a radar station being set up to give early warning of enemy attack, while in 1940 work began on the construction of an RAF night fighter station on Predannack Down, to protect the nearby ports of Falmouth and Penzance. In May 1941, men of the 70th Battalion, Oxfordshire & Buckinghamshire Light Infantry, were moved to Predannack in order to provide airfield defences; they found themselves living in a 'home of bog' within three miles of the Lizard and 'almost in the front line, with nothing but sea between them and the Germans in Brittany, eighty miles away'.

The new airfield was opened in 1941 as part of the Portreath Sector, and by 1944 it was being used by no less than five RAF squadrons, the aircraft stationed there being a mixture of Mosquitoes, Spitfires, Wellingtons and Liberators - the latter being allocated to a Czech Squadron. Aviation facilities continued to develop throughout World War II, and in the early part of 1944 a large tract of land near Helston was acquired by the Navy for the construction of an air station. This aerodrome was not completed until after the war but, in the long term, the opening of RNAS Culdrose on 17th April, 1947 was of immense importance to Helston and the Lizard (*see also Chapter Four*).

The construction of RNAS Culdrose brought much extra traffic to the Helston branch during the later stages of the war, Gwinear Road, Nancegollan and Helston stations being used for that purpose. At the same time, movements of service personnel to RAF Predannack and other establishments in the area ensured that branch passenger trains were often packed with sailors or airmen. This traffic continued for several years after 1945, special trains being run as required (especially during the Christmas and Easter holiday periods).

Ordinary passenger services were reduced at the start of the war, but as the war effort got into its stride some of the missing trains were restored. In November 1939 the basic branch train service provided only six up and six down workings, with departures from Helston at 7.50, 9.20, 11.59 am, 1.25, 4.25 and 6.10 pm, while in the opposite direction, southbound trains left Gwinear Road at 8.40, 9.50 am, 12.40, 2.45, 5.20 and 7.55 pm.

The most interesting feature of wartime operation was the appearance - albeit sporadically - of an armoured train. Designed to counteract Britain's acute shortage of conventional armoured vehicles in the aftermath of Dunkirk, this unusual ensemble consisted of an ex-Great Eastern Railway 'F4' class 2-4-2T

Gwinear Road station, looking west on 2nd September, 1936. An unidentified 2-6-2T is in the branch platform with a Helston working. *Lens of Sutton Collection*

flanked by two low-sided general purpose wagons and two LMS steel 20 ton coal wagons. The train was protected by quarter inch steel plate and equipped with rifles, machine guns and naval six pounders; when on patrol it carried a crew of 26, including gunners, wireless operators and locomen.

The war came to an end in 1945, but the 'emergency' train service established during the years of conflict remained in operation for several more months. In April 1946 local travellers were given a choice of seven up and seven down trains, with departures from Helston at 7.50, 9.20, 11.50 am, 1.25, 3.30, 4.15 and 7.05 pm. Balancing down wordings left Gwinear Road at 8.40, 9.55 am, 12.40, 2.30, 4.15, 5.35 and 8.35 pm respectively. An additional late train had been restored by 1947, and the October 1947 public timetable reveals that daily train services consisted of eight up and eight down workings. There was, however, very little attempt to cater for summer holiday traffic, and the full summer Saturday timetable was not reintroduced until the following year. The 1948 summer timetable provided eight trains each way, but on Saturdays the service was increased to a grand total of 10 up and 12 down workings - a level of service comparable to that provided in the summer of 1939.

The British Railways passenger timetable for 1948.

Chapter Four

Through the Window:
The Route Described

Having taken the story of the Helston line up to the end of the Great Western era, it would now be appropriate to take an imaginary journey over the route in order to study the track and infrastructure of this attractive Cornish branch line in greater detail. Readers should therefore imagine themselves aboard a Helston train in the branch platform at Gwinear Road; the year will be *circa* 1960, and we will take a journey over the railway as it would have appeared on the eve of its impending demise.

Gwinear Road

Gwinear Road, the junction for branch services to Helston, was an entirely rural station with up and down platforms for main line traffic and an additional platform face for branch trains, the down platform being an island, with tracks on either side. There were no run-round facilities or bays for branch trains and, for this reason, it was necessary for incoming branch workings to run-round on the main line – 'wrong line' operation being unavoidable in this situation.

The evolution of Gwinear Road station was a long, and somewhat complex process that had started as far back as the 1840s, when regular passenger services commenced running on the Hayle Railway. Contemporary press reports make no mention of a station at Gwinear, though it is conceivable that trains may have called to pick-up or set-down passengers on an informal basis. However, if that was indeed the case, the facilities provided would have been primitive in the extreme – the 'station building' (if it existed) being no more than a simple hut or shack. Gwinear Road appears in the public timetables for the first time in 1852, suggesting that the first 'proper' station had been brought into use under West Cornwall Railway auspices; in those early days, the station consisted of a single passenger platform on the down side of the line, together with a run-round loop for goods traffic, and a group of sidings on the down side.

Important developments took place during the 1880s, when the Helston Railway was constructed and linked to the main line via 'a siding near the Gwinear Road station'. The siding in question would clearly have been one of the goods sidings on the down side, which would otherwise have obstructed the route of the proposed branch line. In its rebuilt form, the station provided two main line platforms, each with a length of 578 ft, together with a 540 ft branch platform on the south, or outer face of the down platform. The West Cornwall main line was doubled between Camborne and Gwinear Road in January 1900, and between Gwinear Road and Angarrack in December 1909.

The main station building, on the down side, was a timber-framed structure with a low-pitched gable roof, and there was a somewhat smaller waiting room on the up platform. The down side buildings featured projecting canopies on

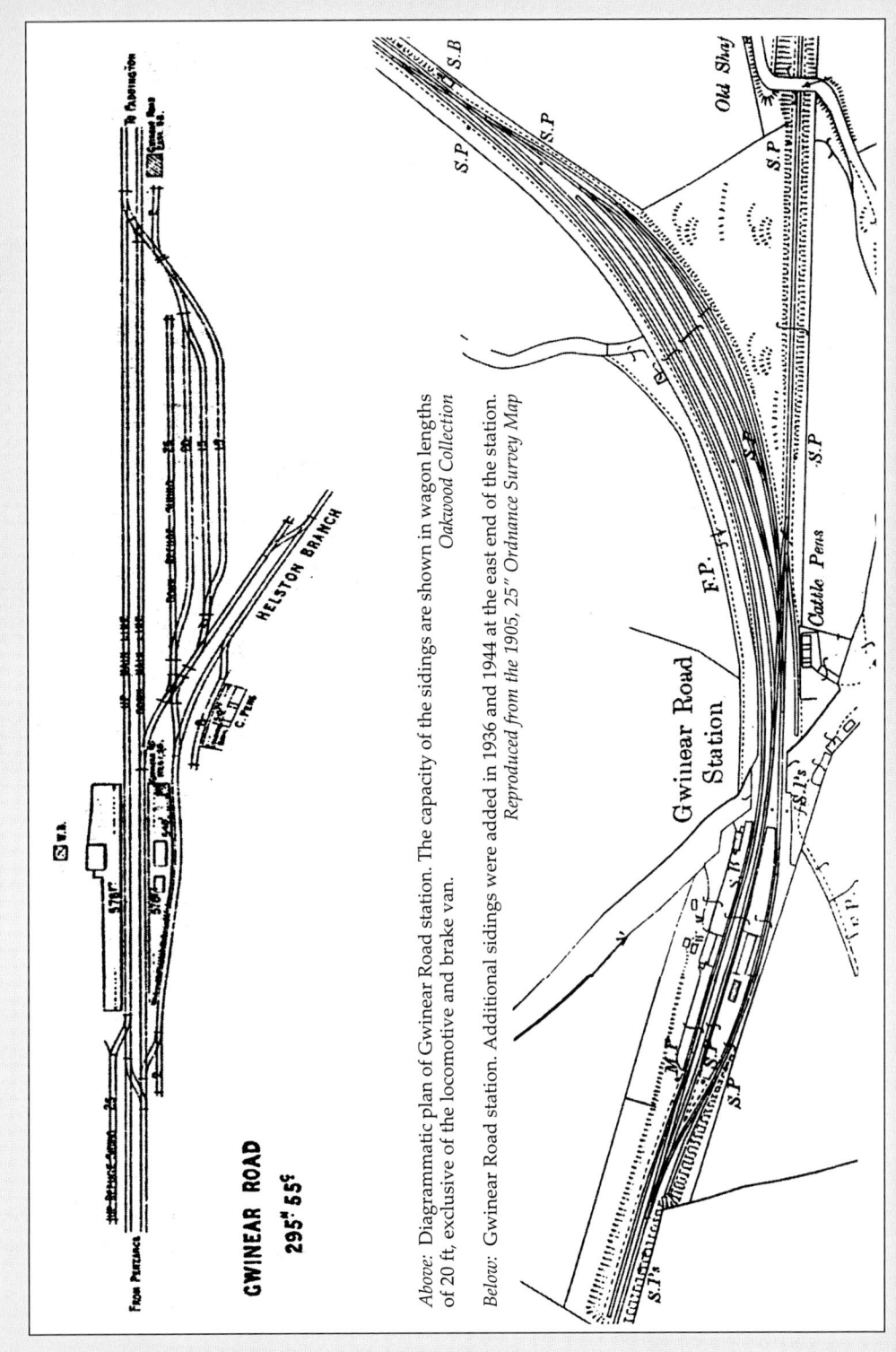

Above: Diagrammatic plan of Gwinear Road station. The capacity of the sidings are shown in wagon lengths of 20 ft, exclusive of the locomotive and brake van.
Oakwood Collection

Below: Gwinear Road station. Additional sidings were added in 1936 and 1944 at the east end of the station.
Reproduced from the 1905, 25" Ordnance Survey Map

THROUGH THE WINDOW : THE ROUTE DESCRIBED 77

Two views of Gwinear Road station, both looking west towards Penzance. Gwinear Road became a station in 1843, when the Hayle Railway introduced its pasenger train service. It passed to the West Cornwall Railway in 1846 and to the Great Western Railway in 1878, and was the station chosen by the Helston Railway as its junction with the main line. Helston branch trains used the outermost face of the down (island) platform. *(Both) Lens of Sutton Collection*

The eastern end of the down platform at Gwinear Road station on 5th September, 1958.
Provenance Unknown

A general view of the up platform at Gwinear Road, *circa* 1960, looking east towards Truro and Paddington. *Lens of Sutton Collection*

'Castle' class 4-6-0 No. 4083 *Abbotsbury Castle* passes through Gwinear Road with an up freight working on 9th April, 1960. *P.Q. Treloar*

'45XX' class 2-6-2T No. 4540 shunts at Gwinear Road. *P.Q. Treloar*

'45XX' class 2-6-2T No. 4570 leaves Gwinear Road with the 10.50 am down service to Helston on 19th September, 1959. *P.Q. Treloar*

'Modified Hall' class 4-6-0 No. 7925 *Westol Hall* leaves Gwinear Road with a down parcels train on 4th July, 1959. *P.Q. Treloar*

both sides, while the up side building boasted a single pitch roof that was continued over the platform as a canopy. Both buildings sported decorative 'groove and hole' valancing, which did much to enliven structures that would otherwise have been of utilitarian weather-boarded construction. A contemporary report, written a few months before the opening of the Helston line, described the internal arrangements as follows:

> On the down platform to Helston the station building will be 64 feet long. The station will comprise booking offices, waiting rooms, ladies' room, lavatories, etc. Adjoining will be a building 30 feet long by 11 feet wide, comprising porters' room, stores for coal, etc. On the up platform will be a building 64 feet long and about 26 feet wide, including verandah.

The up side building was subsequently extended at its eastern end, in order to provide a greater length of platform covering on the eastbound platform. It is of interest to note that the contractors responsible for the new station buildings at Gwinear Road were Messrs Thomas Olver & Sons of Falmouth - a well-known local building firm which had been established in 1811. Olvers had erected numerous public buildings in Cornwall, and had also built the Cornwall Railway stations at Lostwithiel, Falmouth, Penryn, Par, St Austell and elsewhere.

The up and down sides were linked by a plate girder footbridge, which was authorized in May 1907 at an estimated cost of £350, although the final cost (May 1909) was £354 16s. 10d. A public road crossed the running lines at an awkward angle at the east end of the passenger platforms and, on a minor point of detail, it is interesting to find that the level crossing gates needed to protect this skew crossing were said to have been the longest in Cornwall!

Gwinear Road had a relatively complex track layout, with sidings on both sides of the running lines. Two dead-end sidings on the up side were used mainly for the loading of potatoes, broccoli or other agricultural traffic, while an extensive array of sidings on the down side of the line were employed primarily for storage and re-marshalling purposes. There were, in addition, long up and down refuge sidings on each side of the main line, and these were frequently used to berth slow moving freight trains that would otherwise have caused delay to more important passenger workings. Extra siding accommodation was authorised on 6th October, 1944 for the Admiralty in connection with the naval air station at Culdrose, this work being completed on 12th December, 1944.

The station was controlled from two standard Great Western signal boxes, Gwinear Road West signal box being sited on the down platform, while Gwinear Road East signal box was situated further along the main line at the eastern extremity of the station complex. Both of these boxes were of the later, hipped-roof pattern, with five-paned windows. The West box was re-sited in 1916, the original West box having been situated at the east end of the up platform.

In January 1907, the GWR Directors authorized the construction of a station master's house on railway-owned land on the south side of the main line, the contract being awarded to Messrs Johnson at a price of £360. Until 1938 the platforms were lit by simple oil lamps, but in later years Gwinear Road was

An interesting feature at Gwinear Road was this outside-framed 'Mink' goods van body, which was used as an office on the up side loading bank. *Pat English*

'Hall' class 4-6-0 No. 4931 *Hanbury Hall* leaves Gwinear Road with an up parcels train on 22nd May, 1959. The Helston branch is visible on the extreme right. *M. Mensing*

THROUGH THE WINDOW : THE ROUTE DESCRIBED

'Grange' class 4-6-0 No. 6808 *Beenham Grange* enters Gwinear Road station with a down stopping train in 1959.
P.Q. Treloar

'45XX' class 2-6-2T No. 4564 passes over the level crossing as it arrives at Gwinear Road with a train from Helston.
P.Q. Treloar

'45XX' class 2-6-2T No. 4577 arrives at Gwinear Road with an up mixed train from Helston.

P.Q. Treloar

'45XX' class 2-6-2T No. 4564 (*left*) and '4575' class 2-6-2T No. 5546 shunt the extensive sidings at Gwinear Road. *P.Q. Treloar*

Prairie tank No. 4564 propels a rake of cattle wagons towards the east end of the yard sidings at Gwinear Road. Cleaned-out cattle wagons were widely used for consignments of broccoli and other seasonal vegetables from west Cornwall. *P.Q. Treloar*

THE HELSTON BRANCH

A detailed view showing the turnout at the north end of Praze station that gave access to the goods siding
Pat English

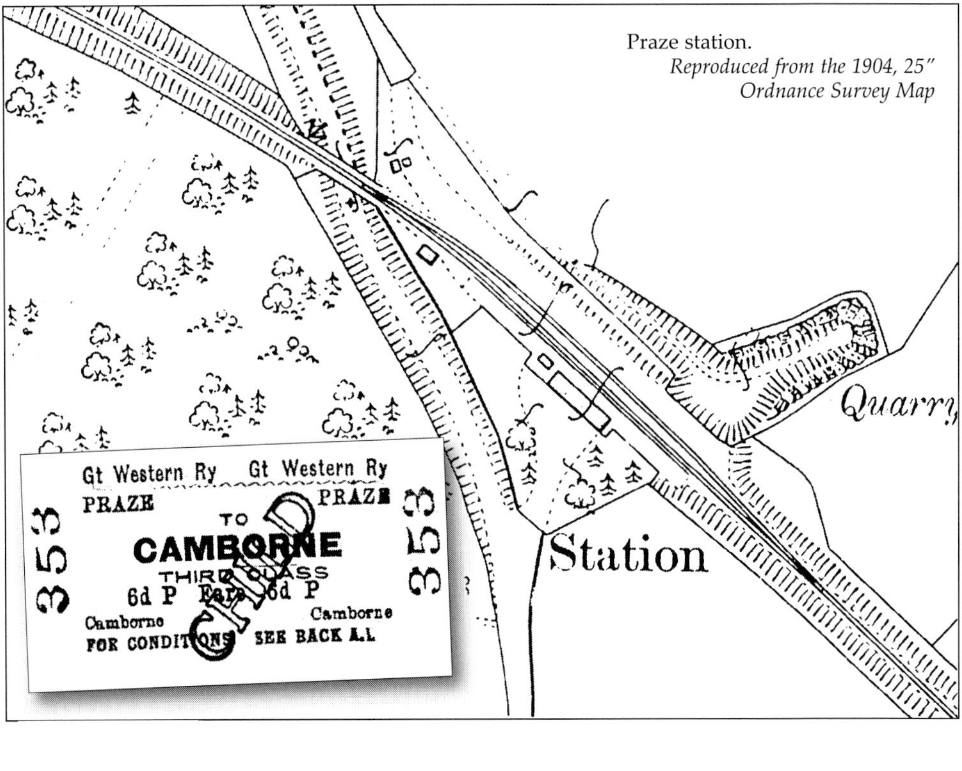

Praze station.
Reproduced from the 1904, 25" Ordnance Survey Map

illuminated by electric lights. Minor details here included the usual cattle pens, loading docks and weigh-house, together with an impressive station nameboard bearing the legend 'GWINEAR ROAD FOR HELSTON, THE LIZARD, MULLION AND PORTHLEVEN'.

Gwinear Road was, on occasions, a busy place, and in addition to the regular arrival and departure of Helston branch trains, its goods sidings were often fully occupied by long rakes of wagons or vans. As the various goods facilities at Gwinear Road were employed mainly for storage or re-marshalling purposes, the amount of originating traffic dealt with here was relatively modest. Indeed, during the 1930s, the station handled no more than 5,000 or 6,000 tons of freight a year. Passenger traffic was fairly healthy, 37,963 tickets being issued in 1913, falling to 20,649 by 1929 and around 14,000 bookings per annum throughout the 1930s. In practice, the apparent decline in the number of passengers can probably be attributed to the increased use of season tickets by regular travellers; in 1938, for instance 13,288 ordinary tickets were issued, together with 98 seasons.

The station provided employment for a labour force of around 14 people. In 1929 these included six porters, three signalmen, two goods shunters, one clerk, one goods guard and a class three station master. Among those employed at this rural junction in the 1930s were booking clerk R.B. Williams, shunter A.J. Mewson and goods guard G. Stephens. Later, around 1960, the staff included goods guard D. Allen, leading porter R.C. Uren, and signalman I.V. Chatsworthy. The station master in the early 1960s was Mr W.D. Richards.

Traffic dealt with at Gwinear Road

Year	Staff	Receipts (£)	Tickets	Parcels	Goods tonnage
1903	10	5,032	22,078	1,503	2,730
1913	13	11,977	37,963	2,773	6,715
1923	13	10,079	28,667	3,994	3,836
1929	15	11,592	20,649	6,098	4,218
1935	14	12,411	14,077	8,503	5,686
1936	14	12,585	13,322	12,716	5,863
1937	14	11,783	14,039	14,423	5,776
1938	14	12,226	13,288	22,579	5,129

Praze

Leaving Gwinear Road, Helston branch trains headed south-eastwards for a short distance before entering a cutting and commencing their initial 1 in 60 climb towards the first mile post. Beyond, the route dipped gently for about one mile and then resumed its 1 in 60 ascent towards the first intermediate station at Praze.

Serving the nearby villages of Crowan and Praze-an-Beeble, Praze was a small, single platform station, situated some 2 miles 68 chains from Gwinear Road. Its modest facilities consisted of a passenger platform on the up side and a single goods siding on the down side of the running line, the siding being

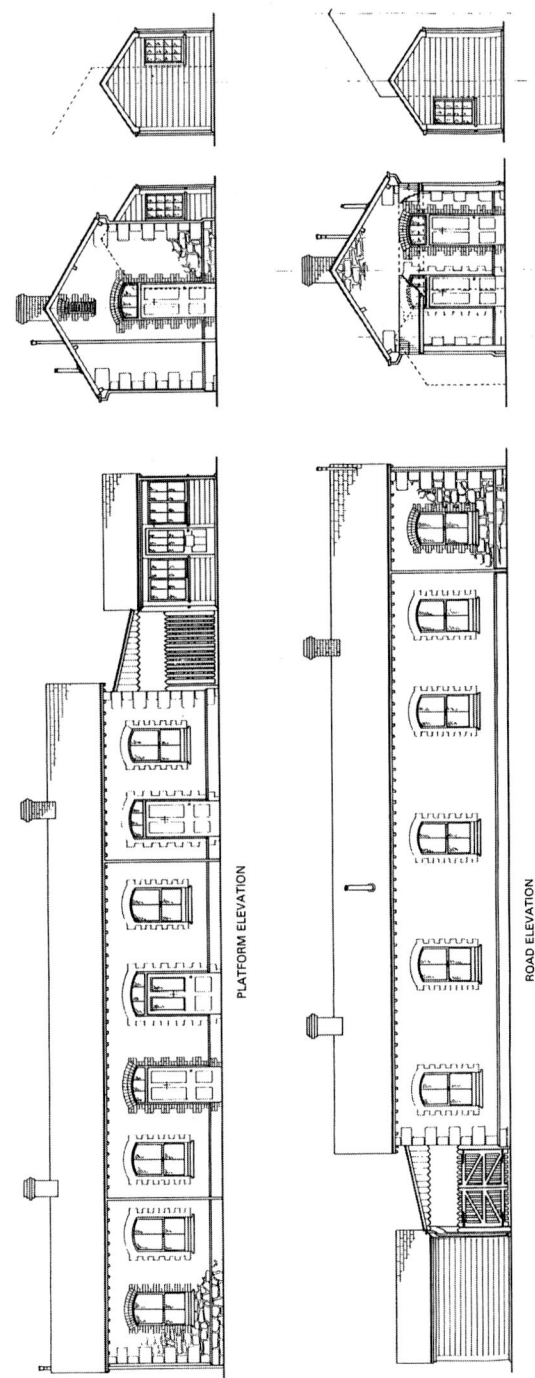

Pat English

Praze station building

Walls in natural stone with the corners faced with squared stone quoins; all doors and windows faced with red brick; chimneys in red brick; roof in slate. Ground frame: timber construction with slate roof. The awning between the two buildings was of timber with a corrugated iron roof.

Praze station originally consisted of a loop with a catch point at each end. This simple layout was modified to produce just one siding, protected by a catch point. The station was situated near the lovely Clowance woods, and conveniently placed for the villages of Praze-an-Beeble and Crowan. *(Both) Lens of Sutton Collection*

Praze station, looking south towards Helston, with the 'mushroom' water tank to the right and the single goods siding to the left. *Pat English*

Praze station, looking north towards Gwinear Road, probably *circa* 1920; the goods siding is still laid with flat-bottomed rail. *Oakwood Collection*

'45XX' class 2-6-2t No. 4563 approaches Praze with an up mixed passenger and freight working.
Lens of Sutton Collection

'4575' class 2-6-2T No. 4577 waits alongside the platform at Praze with a down branch train on 5th September, 1958. *Provenance Unknown*

A brick-built platelayers' hut at the north end of Praze station.

Pat English

Two photographs of the rear of Praze station, with the lower view showing the gated entrance to the platform.

(Both) Pat English

used mainly for wagonload traffic. The gable-roofed building was constructed of local stone, with red brick door and window surrounds; a 3,000 gallon centre-pillar 'mushroom' water tank stood at one end of the platform, and the entire station was situated on an embankment, with a road underbridges at the north end.

There was no signal box, as such, at Praze, and the simple track layout was controlled from a small wooden ground frame hut that was sited on the platform beside the station building. The lever frame could only be operated in conjunction with the electric train staff, which remained locked in the frame until the levers were restored to the normal position.

Other details at Praze included a red brick shed behind the ground frame, a small platelayers' hut on the up side of the running line, and a weigh-house in the tiny goods yard. The station was situated in picturesque, well-wooded surroundings, and in summer time the platform was enlivened by some attractive floral displays. The station nameboard was, unusually, of blue vitreous enamel with white letters, while at night the platform was lit by oil lamps in tapered glass lanterns.

Praze changed little over the years - the only significant alteration being the removal of a single turnout in the years following World War II; this simple operation turned the original loop siding into a dead-end spur, which was entered from the north end.

Praze was the least important intermediate station on the Helston branch, and in pre-Grouping days it issued only 8,000-9,000 tickets per annum. This meagre figure had dropped to 5,793 passenger bookings in 1930, and 3,882 by 1938. Goods tonnage amounted to around 1,000 tons of goods per annum. A limited amount of livestock was dealt with, 18 wagon loads of cattle being received or dispatched in 1923, though in 1933 only two wagon loads were dealt with.

Although only a minor stopping place, Praze was, at one time, considered important enough to have its own station master, and in the early 1900s, this position was filled by Thomas H. Sowell, who had started his career at Ivybridge and later became station master at Bugle, on the Newquay branch. A later station master was Walter G. Lawry, who was in charge of Praze around the time of World War I; the staffing establishment at that time consisted of just two men - a class five station master and one class two porter.

Traffic dealt with at Praze

Year	Staff	Receipts (£)	Tickets	Parcels	Goods tonnage
1903	1	986	8,551	904	1,393
1913	2	1,173	10,306	2,083	1,693
1923	2	1,975	8,073	1,700	1,666
1930	2	1,943	5,793	1,614	2,324
1932	1	1,438	5,700	2,259	1,306
1936	1	1,681	4,195	6,135	920
1937	1	1,782	4,583	8,351	1,002
1938	1	2,318	3,882	14,002	933

Nancegollan Signal Box

Lower storey: red brick. Upper storey: timber. Roof: slate.

Pat English

Nancegollan

From Praze, the single track railway continued to climb but, having surmounted its summit the route began to fall steadily, the steepest gradients on this section being at 1 in 60 and 1 in 65. To the left, travellers could glimpse the village of Crowan, with its attractive granite church dedicated to Saint Crewenna while, in the distance, Crowan Beacon rose over 700 ft above mean sea level.

Still heading southwards, trains continued towards Nancegollan, passing *en route* the site of Nancegollan Loop and its attendant signal box (4 miles 62 chains), which had been opened on 25th May, 1908 to provide extra line capacity at a time of increasing passenger and freight traffic. It remains a matter of conjecture why this facility was not provided at Nancegollan station, a quarter of a mile further on - the likeliest explanation being that, back in 1887, the Board of Trade Inspector had stipulated that Nancegollan station should not be a crossing place. In the event, Nancegollan loop had a relatively short life, and it was abolished when a crossing loop was finally brought into use at Nancegollan station on 19th September, 1937.

Nancegollan, the most important intermediate station on the branch, was an isolated stopping place situated in the centre of a former tin mining area, some 5 miles 9 chains from Gwinear Road. Until the 1930s, its layout had incorporated just one platform on the up side, but in 1937 the GWR remodelled the entire layout. The new works carried out at that time included the provision of up and down platforms, a passing loop, a new signal box and a lengthened road overbridge which spanned several tracks on a combination of stone arches and steel girder spans. At the same time, the Great Western demolished the original station building and added increased siding and wharfage accommodation for broccoli and other freight traffic. The work was authorized in 1935 and completed on 19th September, 1937.

The rebuilt station incorporated long loop lines for passenger and freight traffic, and a new station building on the down side. The new building was a traditional, brick-built structure with a low-pitched roof clad in grey slate; a projecting canopy graced the platform frontage, and the windows had concrete lintels. Internally, the new station building provided the usual passenger and staff facilities, toilets for both sexes and a parcels office. A small brick shed, sited immediately to the right of the main building (when viewed from the platform), was used as a lock-up for small goods and sundries traffic. These buildings were painted in the usual GWR brown and cream livery.

Other buildings at Nancegollan included a standard Great Western signal cabin and a small waiting shelter on the up platform. The signal box was sited immediately to the north of the up platform. Like the station building, this brick-and-timber cabin was of traditional design, with a gable roof and five-pane 'high visibility' windows. Its external dimensions were approximately 20 ft by 12 ft at ground level. The neighbouring waiting shelter was an open-fronted, wood and galvanised iron structure, measuring approximately 24 ft by 9 ft.

There was an extensive goods yard on the up side. This contained six dead-end sidings, one of which had been specially installed as a private siding to deal

Nancegollan Station Building and Store

Station building: walls, red brick with bull-nosed blue brick on the four corners only: plinth, blue brick: roof; slate. Store: red brick with slate roof. The non-standard window on the road elevation replaced a double door (shown by dotted lines on the drawing), the lower wall and plinth being completed in new red brick. An early photograph suggests that the original station building here may have been an identical mirror-image to that existing at Praze on closure.

Pat English

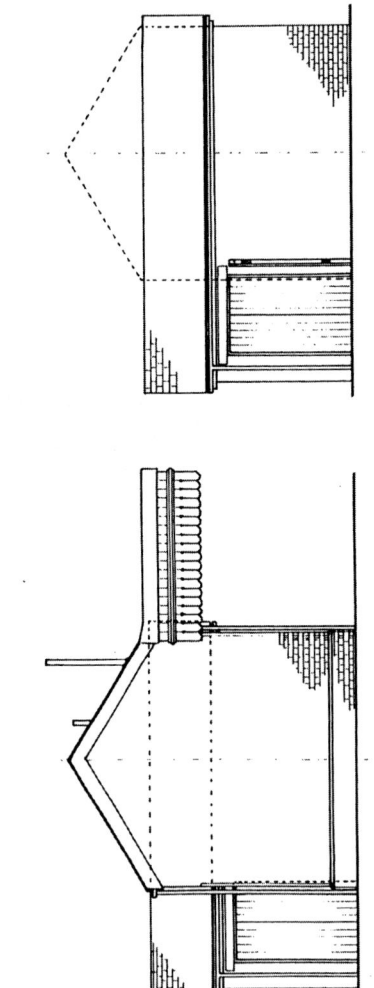
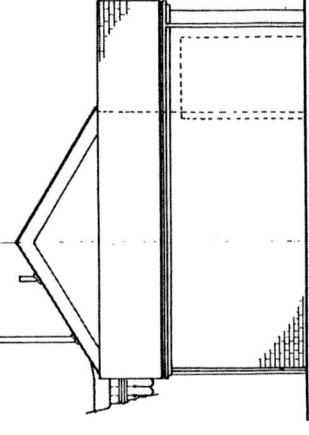
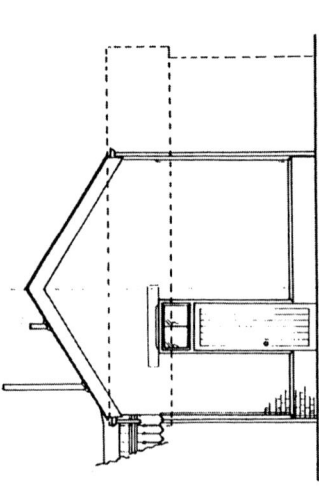

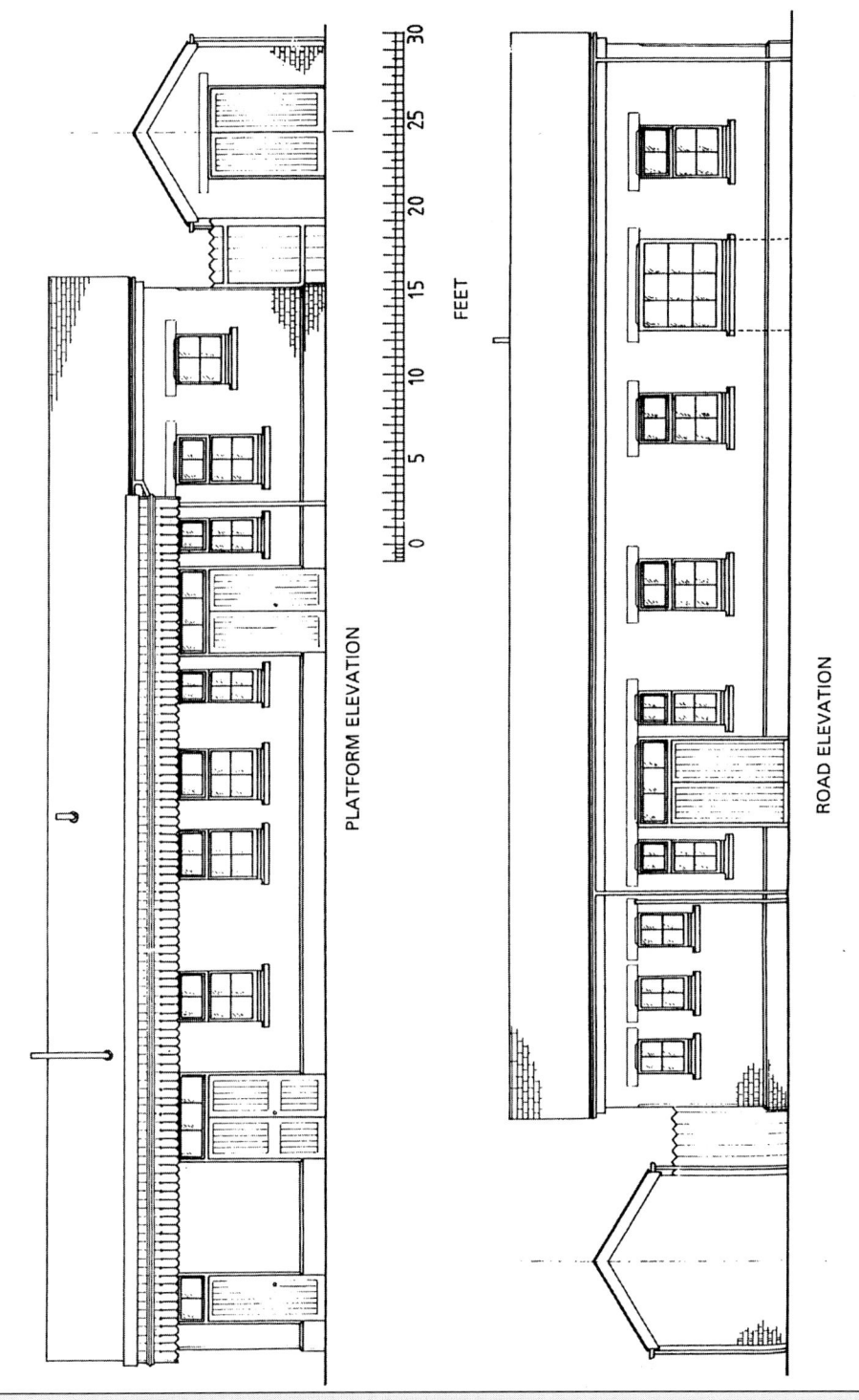

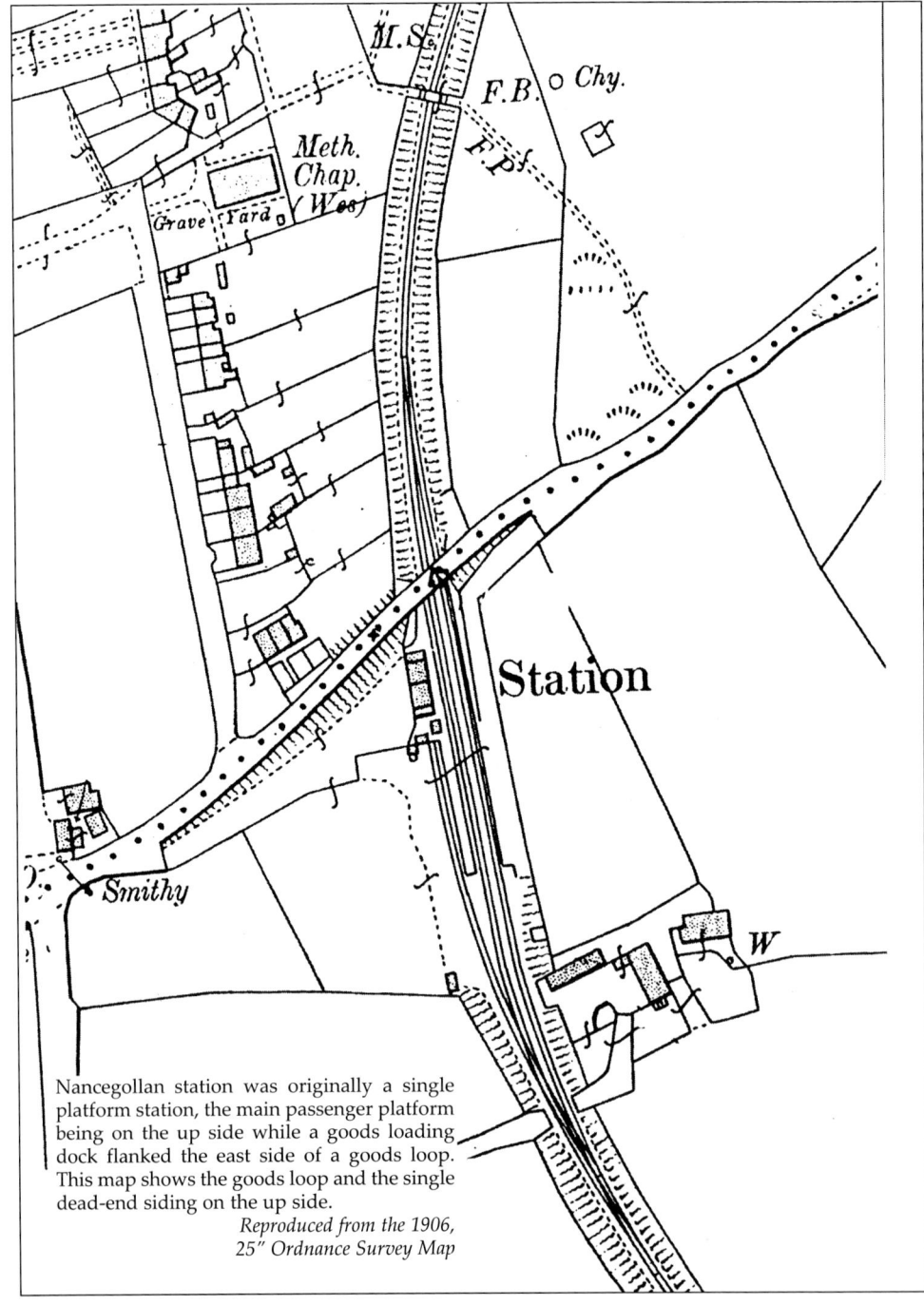

Nancegollan station was originally a single platform station, the main passenger platform being on the up side while a goods loading dock flanked the east side of a goods loop. This map shows the goods loop and the single dead-end siding on the up side.

Reproduced from the 1906, 25" Ordnance Survey Map

THROUGH THE WINDOW : THE ROUTE DESCRIBED

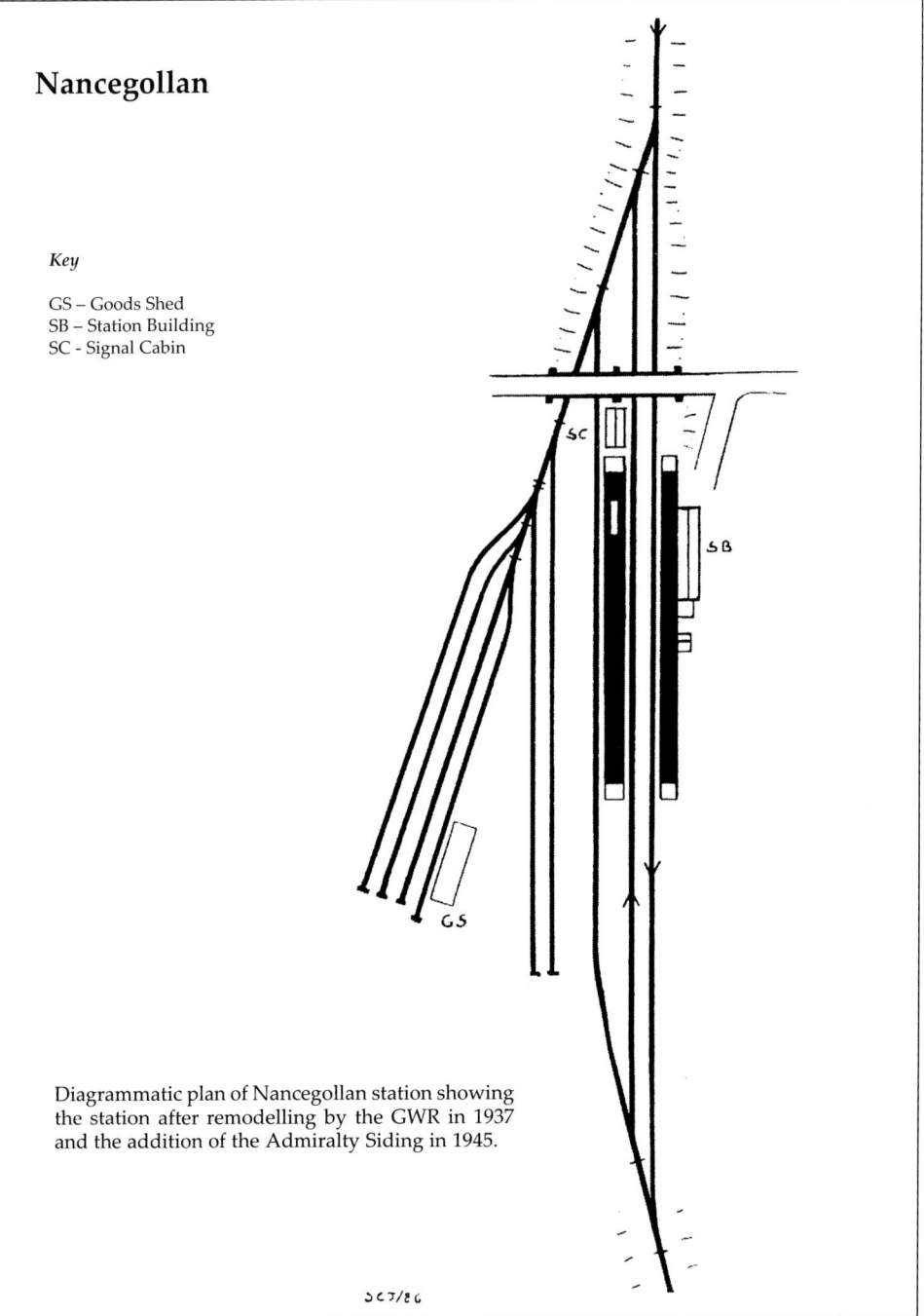

Nancegollan

Key

GS – Goods Shed
SB – Station Building
SC - Signal Cabin

Diagrammatic plan of Nancegollan station showing the station after remodelling by the GWR in 1937 and the addition of the Admiralty Siding in 1945.

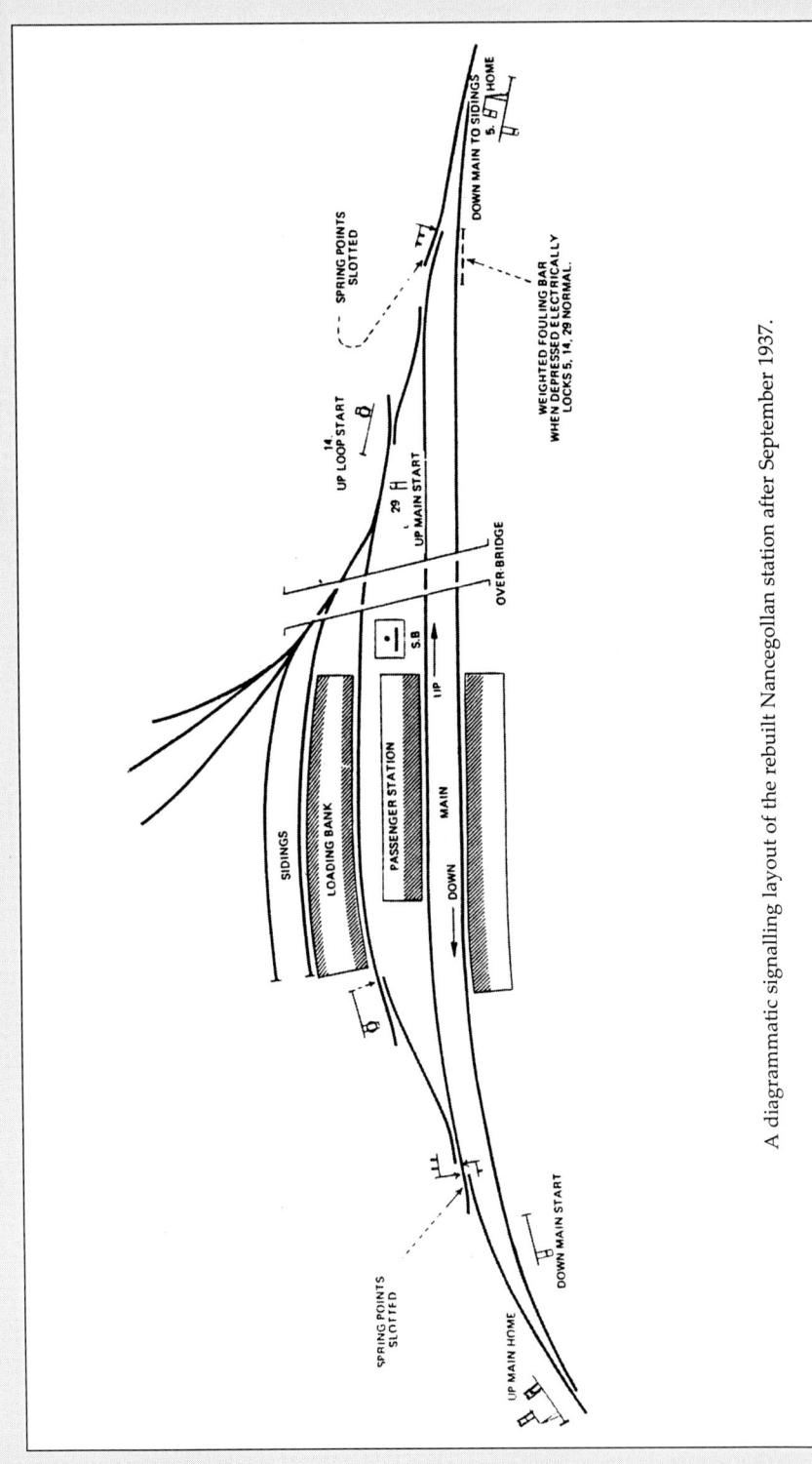

A diagrammatic signalling layout of the rebuilt Nancegollan station after September 1937.

Above: Two views of Nancegollan station, looking north towards Gwinear Road, and showing the GWR signal box erected in 1937 (*left*).
Lens of Sutton Collection

Right: A closer view of the standard GWR signal box at Nancegollan, photographed from the rear on 25th May, 1963.
Pat English

Two views of the brick-built station building at Nancegollan which was the second to be built – the original having been swept away when the station was remodelled by the GWR in 1937; the original building had been very similar to that at Praze. *(Both) Pat English*

Former GWR family and invalid saloon No. 925 in use as a store in Nancegollan goods yard. This vehicle was built to diagram G33 in 1903 under lot 1027.   *Pat English*

with airfield construction traffic during World War II. The 'Admiralty Siding' was authorized on 6th October, 1944 at an estimated cost of £3,045, and the work was completed on 30th December, 1945. The siding was purchased by BR in 1954.

The yard was equipped with a spacious loading bank, and there was a modern goods warehouse, together with a number of old coach or wagon bodies that provided additional storage capacity. One of these venerable vehicles was a Dean clerestory (No. 9025), which had been built to diagram G33 as a family saloon in 1903 under Lot 1027. It was moved to Nancegollan in 1946 and set up on suitable foundations for use as storage accommodation by Messrs Silcox & Sons, who agreed to pay a rent of £1 6s. 8d. per calendar month

The station served a large agricultural area embracing the villages of Nancegollan, Breage, Godolphin, Carleen, Chynhale and Crowntown; it was also conveniently situated for the small, but busy fishing port of Porthleven. Nancegollan was the nearest station to Treverno, the home of William Bickford-Smith, the Chairman of the Helston Railway Company and Member of Parliament for the Truro/Helston division from 1885 until 1892. The station dealt with heavy loadings of broccoli and cauliflower traffic in the days before road haulage became so competitive. On 1st January, 1903 it became a ticket collecting station for passengers travelling to Helston.

In common with other country stations, Nancegollan had a succession of station masters over the years, among them Philip Hancock, who was in charge during the Edwardian period around 1910. In the inter-war years, around 1935, the local station master was A.C. Knight, but he later moved to Grampound Road, his place at Nancegollan being taken by Mr W. Dawe who had transferred from Princetown. Those employed at the station during Mr Dawe's period of office included signalmen C.W. Sheppard and H.W. Oxenham, and porters F.G. Pearce, A. Wakeman, A.E. Carter and J. Wiltshire. Mr Wiltshire subsequently moved to Ashburton as a porter-signalman, while Mr Pearce transferred to Laira as a shunter in 1937. The staff employed at Nancegollan in the British Railways period included porter H.B. Pooley, signalman W. Chappell, and checkers E.D. Treloar and E. Bone - all of whom worked at the station around 1960.

With desolate moors and abandoned tin mines on all sides Nancegollan was not perhaps the best place in which to spend one's summer holidays, but there was, nevertheless, a camping coach on one of the goods sidings, and this vehicle could by hired by holidaymakers for periods of one or two weeks between

A general view of Nancegollan station from the road overbridge, *circa* 1950s. The cattle wagons beside the loading bank would have been carrying broccoli or other vegetables *Pat English*

A detailed view showing the rear elevation of Nancegollan station. *Pat English*

A general view of Nancegollan station looking south towards Helston; a departing train can be glimpsed at the top left of the picture. The commodious goods yard at this station was sometimes used for 'overflow' traffic from Helston, and for consignments to and from RNAS Culdrose.
Lens of Sutton Collection

'45XX' class 2-6-2T No. 4552 shunts a broccoli van in Nancegollan goods yard in 1960. Notice the weigh bridge to the right.
P.Q. Treloar

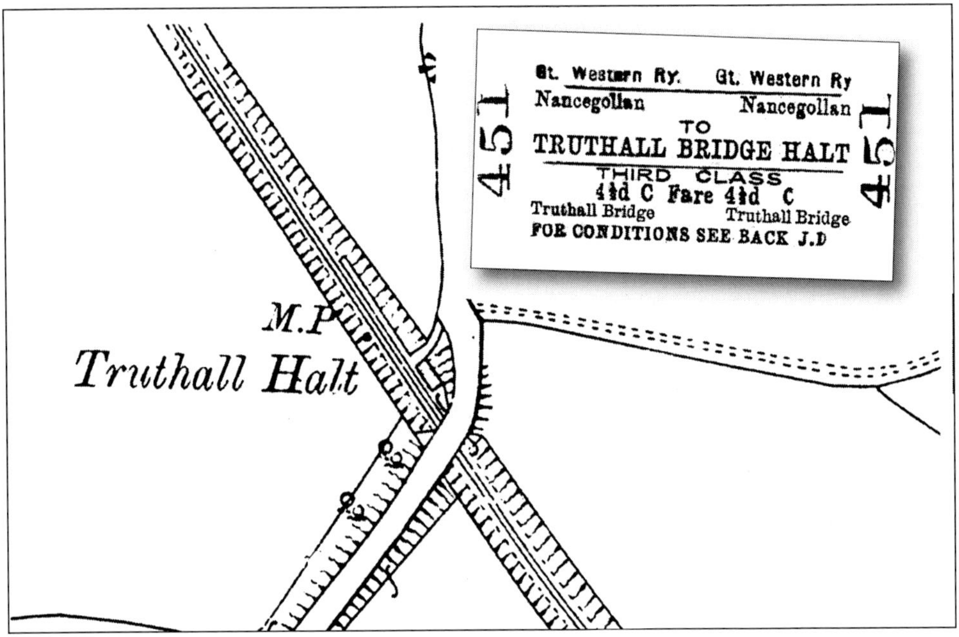

Truthall Halt. *Reproduced from the 1906, 25" Ordnance Survey Map*

A view showing Truthall Halt, looking north towards Gwinear Road, probably during the 1920s.

Oakwood Collection

April and October. Demand for camping coaches usually exceeded the accommodation available, and campers wishing to rent the coaches were asked to buy 'not less than four adult ordinary return tickets for a six-berth' or 'six ordinary return adult rail tickets for an eight-berth coach'. The coaches were equipped with cutlery, cooking utensils and other basic items, but holidaymakers were expected to use the nearby station buildings for water and 'ablution' facilities. The Nancegollan camping coach could be booked for either one or two weeks.

In the early 1900s, the station issued about 10,000 tickets per annum, 9,239 tickets being sold in 1903, rising to 10,819 in 1913, and then falling slightly to 9,272 in 1923. However, in that same year, 39 season tickets were issued, suggesting that the small number of regular travellers may have preferred to pay their travelling expenses in this convenient way. When one considers that GWR season tickets were available for periods of one, three, six or twelve months, it follows that the 39 season ticket holders could have been making as many as 9,360 return journeys each year in addition to the station's ordinary bookings (assuming 39 annual season ticket holders travelling on a daily basis). Thus, in the early 1920s, it could be argued that Nancegollan was a comparatively busy station dealing with up to 18,000 passengers per annum. There was, thereafter, a gradual decline in the number of passenger bookings, and by the later 1930s Nancegollan was issuing around 4,000 ordinary single and return tickets per annum, together with a variable number of season tickets; in 1937, for instance, the station sold 4,716 ordinary tickets and 56 seasons.

The amount of freight traffic handled at Nancegollan was relatively modest; in 1913, for example the station dealt with 3,218 tons of freight, rising to around 5,000 tons per annum during the early 1930s, and decreasing to 3,400-4,000 tons during the final years of that decade.

Traffic dealt with at Nancegollan

Year	Staff	Receipts (£)	Tickets	Parcels	Goods tonnage
1903	2	3,024	9,239	10,513	1,915
1913	4	3,653	10,819	6,796	3,218
1923	5	6,687	9,272	8,675	4,650
1929	5	6,808	7,036	8,432	5,768
1935	5	8,648	4,411	12,061	4,056
1936	5	10,192	4,831	16,894	3,280
1937	5	9,337	4,716	16,707	3,491
1938	5	10,982	4,056	20,698	4,039

Truthall Halt

Leaving Nancegollan, down trains entered a valley and, passing beneath a road overbridge, they rapidly approached the Cober River. Twisting and turning, the line ran through a series of cuttings and, running beneath a further road overbridge, trains coasted downhill on a 1 in 60 falling gradient. Some of the cuttings on this section of the line were excavated through 'solid granite of a particularly hard kind'; the best stone was utilized for building the stations,

Two views of Truthall Halt in the British Railways period. Truthall Halt was opened on 3rd July, 1905, and had its name changed to Truthall Platform in July 1906. Set in the midst of the country, without a dwelling house in sight, it was evidently provided for the convenience of the villagers of Trannack and for the residents of Truthall Manor. It consisted of a galvanised iron shed on a wooden platform long enough to accommodate one coach only. *(Both) Lens of Sutton Collection*

while the remainder provided a useful source of 'bottom ballast' during the construction of the railway. Southwards, the route meandered into the Cober Valley as trains approached Truthall Halt, the next stop, which was seven miles from the junction.

Opened in July 1905, this simple halt, which served the residents of Truthall Manor and people living in nearby Trannack, consisted of a cinder-and-sleeper platform, just 84 feet in length, on the down side, together with a 'pagoda' shed, a name board and a single oil lamp. The 'pagoda' shelter was built of corrugated iron, and its overall dimensions, at ground level, were approximately 19 ft by 8 ft. The platform was faced with old sleepers and buttressed with lengths of old Barlow rails that had been discarded after they had proved so unsatisfactory on the West Cornwall main line during the 1850s. Passengers wishing to alight here were asked to sit in the rearmost coach, so that the train did not have to draw up at the short platform.

When first opened, this un-staffed stopping place had officially been known as Truthall Halt, but in July 1906 its name was changed to Truthall Platform. Later, however, the earlier name was re-introduced, and in the British Railways era the single nameboard displayed the words 'TRUTHALL HALT'. No sidings or other facilities were ever provided at this remote place, which remained throughout its life the smallest and least important station on the Helston branch.

Helston

From Truthall Halt, trains headed due east as they approached the six-arched Cober viaduct - the principal engineering feature en route to Helston (7 miles 64 chains). Passengers in the train from Truthall to Helston experienced the fastest run of their journey as they travelled over a falling gradient of 1 in 60 and the first part of a horse-shoe bend, before crossing the slightly-curved viaduct and accelerating to take the rise of 1 in 60 on the Helston side. This run, much enjoyed by the younger element, particularly the pupils of the grammar school, was governed by strict speed restrictions, and was of course entirely safe. The experience of running down hill towards the soaring granite viaduct was vividly recalled by Pat English who, in the May 1967 *Model Railway Constructor*, described the journey as follows:

> From Truthall the line swept downwards in a tight horse-shoe curve to cross the Cober Valley at its most practical point. The crossing of the valley was accomplished on a six-arch granite viaduct of typical Cornish design, ninety feet above the valley with a fourteen feet wide trackbed. Since the track ran downwards at 1 in 60 and 1 in 77 to meet the viaduct from both directions, and since the curves on both sides were quite severe, a run on this section by a train trying to make up lost time was often more exhilarating than soothing.
>
> To those of us who were in our youth, when the vision of the next world is perhaps not so pressing as it is in later life, a smart run onto the viaduct and the charging gallop up the gradient on the other side, was always the highlight of the journey. But to the unsuspecting traveller who, unhappy with the violent and erratic motion of the train, looked out of the window to find himself emerging abruptly from a cutting at an apparently appalling velocity and being thrown bodily over the yawning chasm of the Cober Valley, the experience must have been considerably chastening.

'45XX' class 2-6-2T No. 4574 coasts across the six-arch Cober viaduct near Helston in September 1957. Engines usually ran with their smokeboxes facing towards Gwinear Road, bunker-first being necessary in the down direction. *P.Q. Treloar*

A panoramic view of the north end of Helston station, looking towards the stone chute siding (*right*) and the single-road engine shed (*left*). *Lens of Sutton Collection*

The viaduct, with its six arched spans, each of 50 ft, had a total length from end to end of 390 ft inclusive of the spandrels. Having crossed the Cober the line entered a further series of cuttings before approaching Helston from the north; here the branch finally terminated on what had once been the eastern side of the town - though in later years Helston spread itself north and eastwards towards the railway. As trains neared their destination they crossed a minor road on an overbridge, beyond which the line passed beneath two more overbridges in quick succession before curving leftwards into Helston station (8 miles 67 chains).

Helston, the most southerly railway terminus on the British mainland, was laid out as a through station, the original intention being that the line would be extended to the Lizard. Only one platform was provided, and the line terminated in a carriage shed about 200 yards beyond the platform, in which were stabled two coaches of a branch spare set.

The station was a classic GWR branch line terminus, with a simple 8-turnout track layout that had changed little since the 1880s; it incorporated a single platform on the up side, an engine release road, and two long goods sidings on the down side. A curious feature of the original track layout was the way in which the engine shed spur had diverged from the engine release road and cut across the station throat before terminating in the single road engine shed. Alterations carried out in May 1915 eliminated this unnecessarily complex piece of trackwork, and in later years locomotives reached their shed by means of a simple turnout from the main line.

Although this modification was of a very minor nature, it entailed the installation of a facing connection on a line used by passenger services, and it was necessary for the changed track layout to be sanctioned by a Board of Trade inspector before the alterations could be brought into use. The new track layout was, in consequence, examined by Lieutenant-Colonel Von Donop RE, of the BoT, on 31st May, 1915, his report being as follows:

31st May, 1915

Sir,

I have the honour to report, for the information of the Board of Trade, that, in compliance with the instructions contained in your minute of 21st May, I have inspected the new works at Helston, on the Great Western Railway.

At the up end of the station an existing through connection has been dispensed with, and a new connection facing to up trains, and leading to an engine shed siding, has been constructed on the single line.

The points and signals are worked from the existing signal box, which contains a frame of 14 levers, all of which are now in use. The interlocking is correct, and the arrangements are satisfactory, and I can recommend the Board of Trade to sanction the new works being brought into use.

I have the honour, etc.,
P.G.Von Donop,
Lt Col., Royal Engineers

A further alteration, carried out around 20 years later, concerned the 'Stone Chute Siding', which had originally diverged northwards near the station

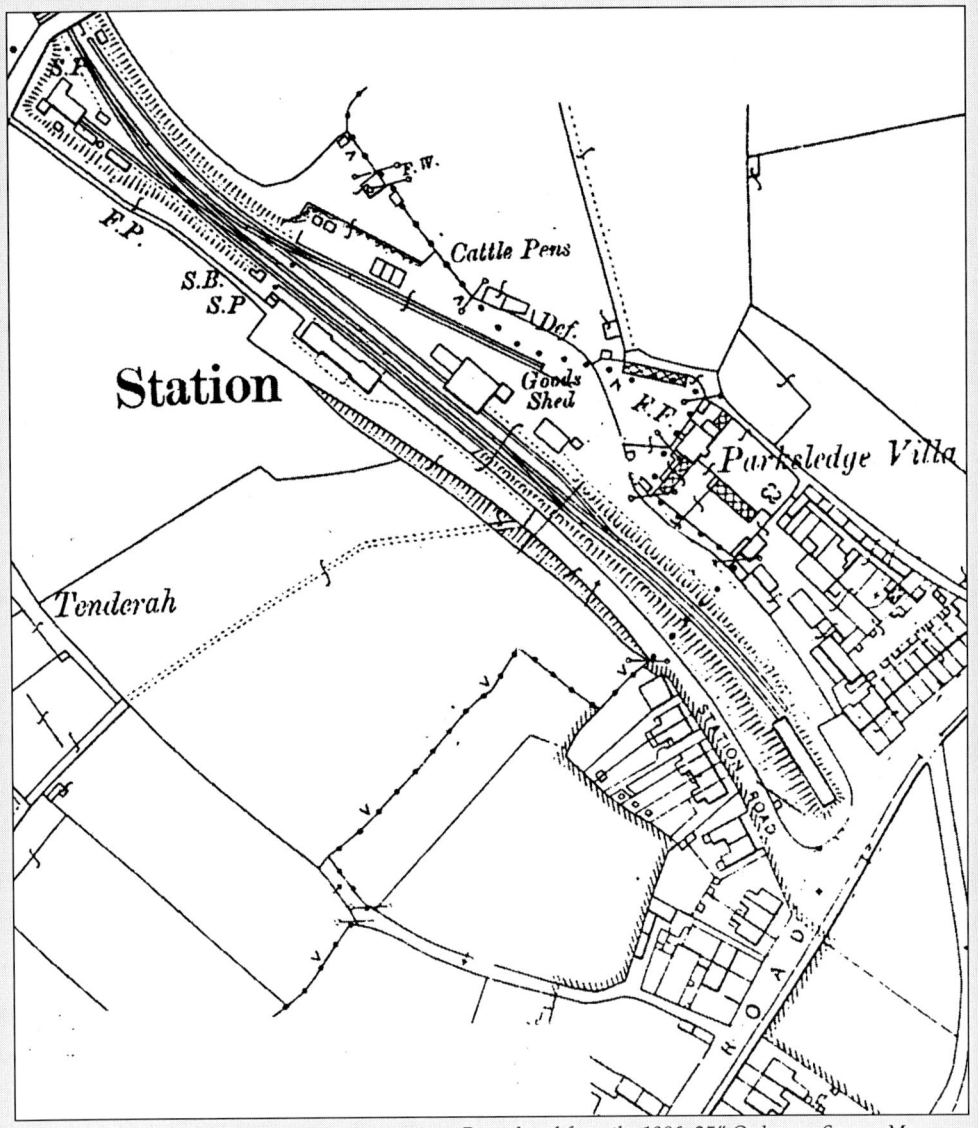

Helston station. *Reproduced from the 1906, 25" Ordnance Survey Map*

A general view of Helston station, probably taken during the 1930s after the lifting of the stone chute siding (*left*). The small locomotive depot can be seen to the right.
Lens of Sutton Collection

Helston station, looking north towards Gwinear Road during the British Railways period. The single-road locomotive shed can be seen to the left. *Oakwood Collection*

A detailed view of the stone chute siding at Helston on 19th May, 1957. This siding was relaid in the BR era to handle an upsurge in Serpentine stone traffic. *Pat English*

'45XX' class 2-6-2T No. 4570 backs three additional coaches onto the 1.15 pm to Gwinear Road, which will then become a six-coach formation. Hopper wagons stand in the stone chute siding on the left, and other goods vehicles pack the nearby goods yard. *P.Q. Treloar*

throat; this short spur was lifted around 1932 but, as mentioned above, it was subsequently reinstated in connection with an upsurge in serpentine traffic in the 1950s, and in British Railways days steel hopper wagons could usually be seen waiting here to be loaded.

The main station building was a solidly-built stone structure with a hipped slated roof. Its overall dimensions were approximately 100 ft by 25 ft at ground level, and there were canopies at both the front and rear, the front (i.e. platform) canopy being a full length attachment that covered the entire facade, and afforded ample protection for waiting passengers. The window and door apertures were slightly arched, and the roof line was punctuated by four prominent chimney stacks.

G.A. Anthony who had once worked at Helston as a clerk, recalled that, internally, the station building incorporated a privately-run refreshment room at its southern end and, next to this, there was a parcels office with an 'inside room' containing train staff instruments and telephones. Moving northwards, one then came to the station master's office, which extended throughout the entire width of the building and connected with the adjacent booking office. Beyond this, there were general and ladies' waiting rooms, together with store rooms and toilets at the northernmost extremity of the building.

The little refreshment room was a particularly pleasant and popular feature of Helston station. This was privately owned for over 50 years and, for a time, was 'presided over by Miss Thomas, who always had a cheerful greeting for every customer and who was well known to the commercial and other regular travellers who used the branch line'. In later years, the refreshment room was extensively used by passengers using the Western National bus services, and by pupils from the nearby grammar and secondary modern schools.

The station building was remarkably similar to that at St Ives, on the neighbouring branch from St Erth, and this suggests that both buildings were based on the same set of plans. The link between these two branch line stations was probably Peter John Margary, who had assisted Sylvanus W. Jenkin during the construction of the Helston branch, and is known to have designed a number of stations and goods sheds throughout the West Country peninsula. P.J. Margary, who had started his career under William Gravatt (an associate of I.K. Brunel) was, for many years, the GWR divisional engineer at Plymouth, and it is interesting to reflect that, through him, the standard gauge Helston branch acquired a style of architecture more usually associated with broad gauge lines built some 50 years earlier.

The station was approached from Helston by a sloping access road, in which were situated a collection of small sheds that were rented-out to traders who forwarded large consignments of dead rabbits to 'up country' destinations such as Sheffield, Birmingham and other industrial cities. The station was built on the side of a hill that dropped perceptibly towards the south and, for this reason, the northern end of the site was enclosed by cuttings while the southern end of the terminus was raised above local ground level on a lofty embankment; there was, therefore, a considerable gradient on the long approach from Godolphin Road (which led, in turn to Wendron Street and thence to Helston town centre). On a footnote, it is worth adding that if the

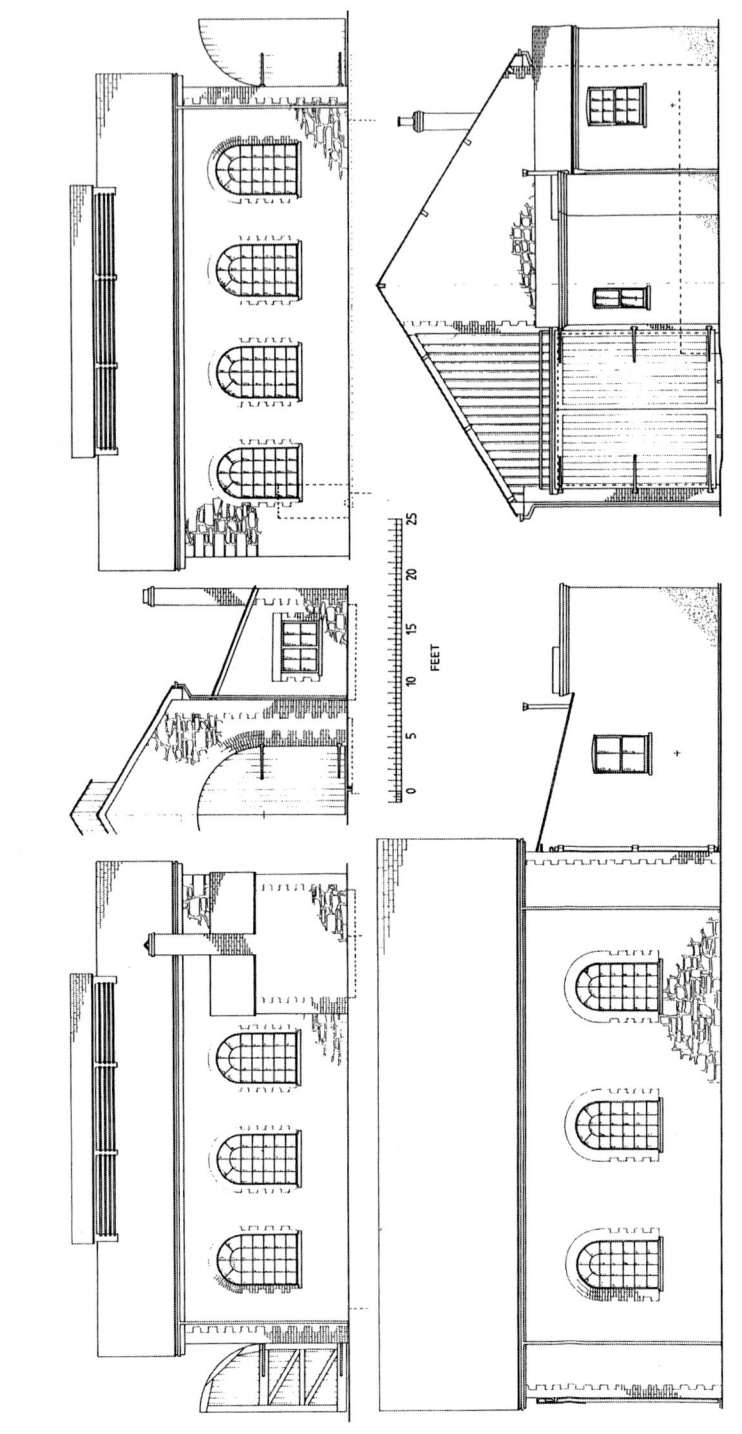

Helston Locomotive Shed

All walls of the lean-to store and of the shed itself (save for the rear wall): natural stone. All windows, doors and corners (save the rear two of the shed): faced in red brick. Chimney: red brick. Roofs: slate. Rear wall and corners of the shed: cement block. Presumably when built the entire structure was in natural stone with brick facings, the rear wall being a later rebuild.

Pat English

The engine shed siding at Helston, with '45XX' class 2-6-2T No. 4563 in attendance. *R.C. Riley*

A useful view of Helston engine shed, photographed from the adjacent overbridge in 1957. The small clerestory and arched windows are clearly seen, while the arrangement whereby the office/mess room abutted the main block is also apparent. This view shows the timber hut beside the shed. *Pat English*

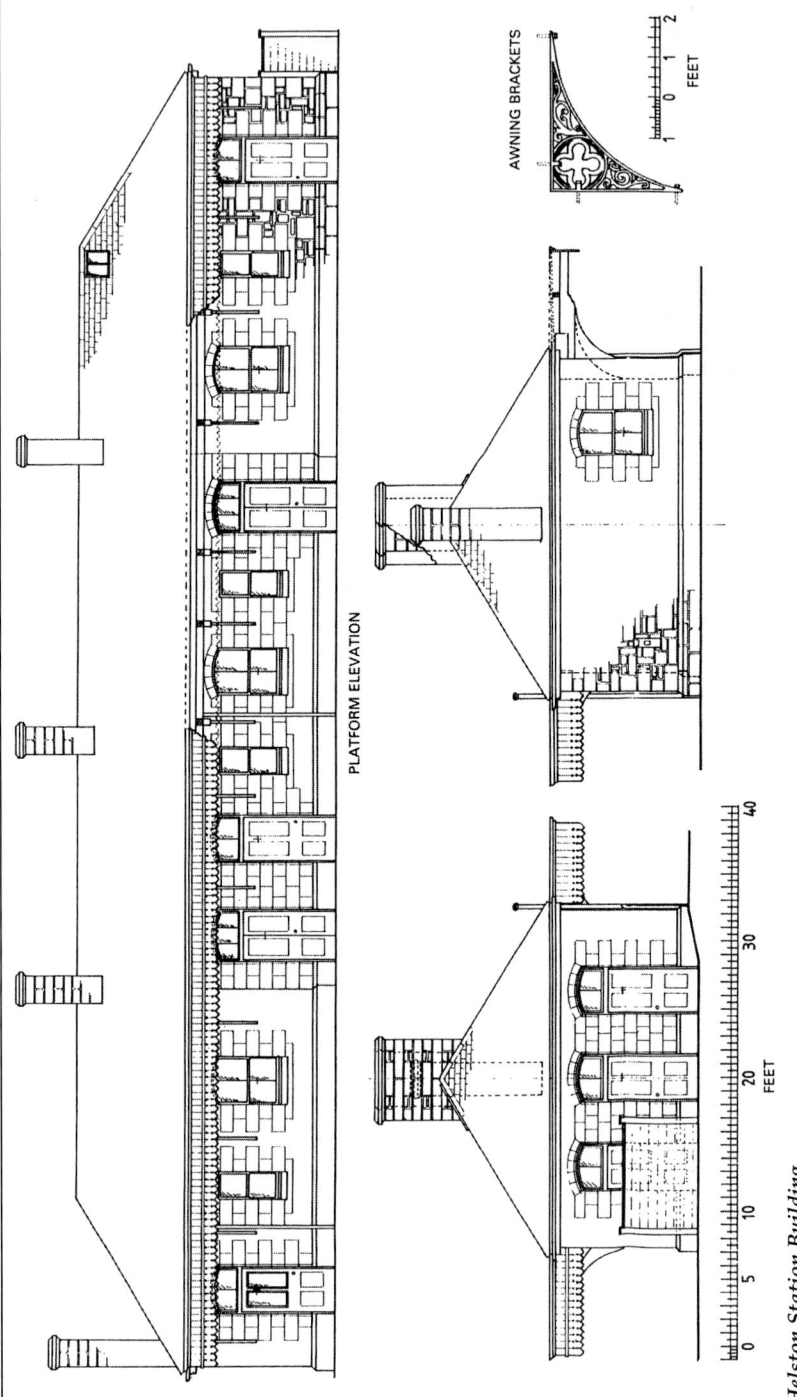

Helston Station Building

All walls and chimneys: dressed granite blocks, regularly coursed on chimneys, window and door surrounds, and on corners; randomly coursed elsewhere. Roof: slate. The south-east wall of the building had a post-box cemented into it, as shown on the drawing. Also fixed to this wall were a number of vertical laths for the attachment of notice boards, advertisements etc. By the date of closure the extreme right-hand door and fanlight shown on the platform elevation had been blocked up and cemented over. The screen around the entrance to the gentlemen's toilet was constructed of pre-cast concrete sections.

Pat English

proposed extension to the Lizard had ever been constructed it would have required substantial earthworks and at least one bridge or viaduct on the east side of Helston.

Helston's goods facilities consisted of a long, raised loading platform that could be used for both side and end loading, with the customary cattle pens, loading gauge, and a mileage siding leading to a typical West Country goods shed; beyond this, there were additional berthing facilities for wagons at the very end of the line. The 'back', or loading bank siding, could accommodate about 25 short wheelbase wagons, and the goods shed/mileage siding could hold a similar number.

Until the early 1930s, a 4-ton fixed yard crane had been available for use when timber, drain pipes or other heavy consignments were loaded or unloaded, while a 2-ton crane served the goods shed - which also had a platform weighing machine. The old yard crane (designated 'FM651') was replaced in 1932, its more powerful successor being a 'new, 6-ton hand crane purchased from Messrs J.H. Wilson (M491)' at a cost of £238.

The solidly-built goods shed was similar to scores of others throughout the western counties. It was a roughly square building, being about 50 ft long and 50 ft wide; internally, the shed contained a spacious loading-platform, with sufficient room for about two standard Great Western vans. Large wooden doorways in each gable enabled railway vehicles to enter the building, while a further opening in the east wall provided a means of access for road vehicles. The shed was constructed of irregular chunks of local stone and lit by boldly-arched windows, three of which were in the west wall, while two more were situated in the east wall on either side of the cart entrance. All of these openings were faced with yellowish-white brickwork that contrasted favourably with the dark grey stonework of the main exterior walls.

The goods shed incorporated a lean-to office at its south end, this otherwise unremarkable structure being distinguished by the addition of a flat-roofed extension, which formed a sort of entrance porch. In British Railways days, the shed had hinged doors at one end and a shutter type door at the other - though when first built the rail entrances had been equipped with sliding doors, which can be glimpsed in many late-Victorian photographs of the station.

A large, corrugated iron building near the goods shed functioned as a 'Road Motor Shed'. This structure had originally sheltered the GWR motor buses, and it was later utilized by the Western National Omnibus Company. The buses were transferred to a new and much larger garage in Clodgey Lane in 1933, but the road motor depot remained in use as a garage for Helston's fleet of railway-owned collection and delivery vehicles.

Until the 1930s, there had been a small weigh bridge suitable for weighing horse-drawn vehicles, but of insufficient capacity for road vehicles. To rectify this deficiency the GWR decided to replace the original weighing machinery with a more modern machine, and in June 1937 the *Great Western Railway Magazine* reported that the 'existing cart weighing machine' at Helston was being replaced by a 'new 20 ton weigh bridge' capable of weighing motor vehicles.

The usual diverse collection of coal wharves and storage sheds was occupied by local coal merchants and agricultural firms, and there was also a large

Above: A view of Helston station from the rear, showing the projecting canopy, which was somewhat smaller than the one provided on the platform side.
Pat English

Right: A detail of the spandrels which supported the awnings at Helston station (*see plan page 118*).
Pat English

abattoir on the loading bank, which was conveniently placed for the quick loading of meat traffic into ventilated or refrigerated vans. A large coal and building merchant's yard also had a direct means of road access to and from railway property. Until about 1928 a large petrol storage tank had been situated at the southern end of the embankment.

The signal box, at the north end of the passenger platform, was originally equipped with a 14-lever frame (including spares), but a larger, 21-lever frame was subsequently installed. This had 11 signal levers, five point levers, two facing point lock levers and spaces for three spares levers. Externally, the two-storey cabin was unusual (though by no means unique) in that it was an example of a Great Western box with vertical match boarding on its upper floor, instead of the standard horizontal weather boarding. Such boxes were characteristic of Great Western practice during the 1890s, when Helston station was first opened.

The terminus was fully signalled with starting signals at the end of the platform, an advanced starter at the station throat, and a home signal for incoming down trains. The latter was, for many years, a simple, single-post signal with just one arm - its one claim to fame being its excessive height. In 1947, an additional bracketed arm was added to the existing home signal so that down freight trains could run straight into the goods sidings. In the 1960s, the lever frame was arranged as follows - these details being slightly different to those in force during the early days:

Signal or Turnout	Lever No.	Lever colour
Down main home signal	1	Red
Down main home siding arm	2	Red
Facing point lock for 4	3	Blue
Down main facing points	4	Black
Run-round loop catch points	5	Black
Run-round loop ground disc	6	Red
Loading bank siding points	7	Black
Loading bank siding ground disc	8	Red
Space	(9)	–
Space	(10)	–
Space	(11)	–
Engine shed ground disc	12	Red
Down main shunting ground disc	13	Red
Facing point lock for No. 15	14	Blue
Engine shed spur points	15	Black
Run-round loop to main points	16	Black
Up starting to engine shed arm	17	Red
Up main shunt ahead arm	18	Red
Up main advanced starting	19	Red
Up main starting signal	20	Red
Ground disc from south sidings	21	Red

As mentioned above, these arrangements were in force at around the time of closure, the lever frame having been renewed in 1958. At one time the number sequence had been slightly different; No. 21, for instance, had controlled the engine shed spur ground disc, while lever No. 12 had worked the points at the

Helston station, looking north towards Gwinear Road, *circa* 1912. *Provenance Unknown*

Helston station, looking south around 1958. The hip-roofed building contained the usual booking office, waiting rooms and office accommodation, together with a privately-run refreshment room. *Lens of Sutton Collection*

THROUGH THE WINDOW : THE ROUTE DESCRIBED

Helston station, looking south on 27th September, 1956. '45XX' class 2-6-2T No. 4570 stands in the station with an up branch train.
R.M. Casserley

A general view of Helston station, *circa* 1958, looking northwards along the single platform, and showing Collett '4575" class 2-6-2T No. 4577 with a down train from Gwinear Road.
Lens of Sutton Collection

'45XX' class 2-6-2T No. 4548 waits in the single platform at Helston during the BR era.
Oakwood Collection

A detailed view of Helston station building, *circa* 1960, looking south.   *Lens of Sutton Collection*

south end of the run-round loop. In general, however, the frame details reproduced here are correct for the post-1947 period, the main signal levers (Nos. 1, 2, 17, 19 and 20) being the same before and after the 1958 alterations.

Turning from the signalling system to the locomotive department, it is perhaps worth mentioning that Helston's single-road engine shed was built to a standard Great Western design that had originated on West Country lines during the broad gauge era. Ashburton shed, opened in 1872, and Moretonhampstead shed, opened in 1866, were remarkably similar, their overall dimensions (45 ft by 23 ft) being marginally greater to accommodate broad gauge engines, whereas the standard gauge shed at Helston measured 43 ft by 21 ft at ground level. All three sheds were built of local stone, with prominently-arched window and door openings, and raised clerestories to facilitate smoke emission.

Helston shed featured a combined office and mess room on the east side, the ground level dimensions of this lean-to structure being 9¼ ft by 8½ ft. The shed was accompanied by a group of ancillary structures including two concrete block-built coaling stages, a platelayers' hut and a standard GWR 'mushroom' water tank that was equipped with a flexible hose from which locomotives could replenish their tanks.

In 1914, the resident locomotive was '517' class 0-4-2T No. 1481, while locomotives allocated to Helston in 1921 included '517' class 0-4-2T No. 1158 and '44XX' class 2-6-2T No. 4403.

Apart from the station building, goods shed and engine shed, the only other 'large' structure at Helston was the carriage shed at the very end of the line. Built of what appeared to be semi-prefabricated timber components, the carriage shed measured approximately 100 ft by 15 ft. Its walls were clad in vertical match boarding, and the low-pitched roof was topped by a shallow clerestory - the overall appearance of the building being somewhat similar to that of a wooden engine shed (the carriage shed was removed during the British Railways era, around 1958).

Minor structures at Helston were of a varied nature, and in addition to the above-mentioned weigh-house, permanent way hut and coal merchants' sheds, there were two small buildings at the north end of the passenger platform. One of these structures was of wooden construction, and functioned as a store, while its companion was built of brick and was used as a staff mess room; the store measured 20 ft by 7 ft, and the mess room was 13½ ft by 9 ft. It seems likely that, when the railway was first opened, the brick building had contained 'hot water apparatus for supplying foot warmers'.

The station was lit by electric light, and platform fittings included the usual Great Western type seats with 'GWR' in their ironwork. There were a number of four-wheel trolleys for the conveyance of parcels or other items, and these were normally parked in the open near the porters' mess room at the north end of the platform.

In staffing terms, Helston gave employment to a variety of grades in the passenger, goods, locomotive and permanent way departments - road motor drivers being a particularly important group at this station. In 1888, the station master had been Lawrence Reed, but he had been replaced by Daniel Silvester

Helston station from the south end of the platform; a '45XX' class 2-6-2T has just arrived with a branch train, and a rake of goods vans occupy the adjacent engine release road. On the extreme left, on the station forecourt, somewhat obscured, is a Western National double-decker bus.
Lens of Sutton Collection

A view of the rarely-photographed southern end of Helston station, showing the pointwork at the end of the run-round loop.
Pat English

by 1906, and at the start of World War I the station master was Frederick William French.

Generally speaking, Helston had a staff of around 20 people during the early 1930s, in addition to locally-based permanent way men and locomotive crews. In March 1929 the staffing establishment comprised one 'class two' station master, three booking clerks, one goods clerk, one general clerk, one parcels porter, one porter-guard, three porters, one goods checker, one goods porter, three motor drivers, two signalmen, two passenger guards and a charwoman. The number of motor drivers was later increased from three to six, in connection with Helston's role as a county lorry centre for the Lizard peninsula, and by the 1930s the staffing establishment had been increased to 22.

Some railway employees moved from station to station in search of higher pay or promotion, but many individuals preferred to remain in one place for much of their working lives. Sainthill Lindsey, the Helston branch passenger guard was clearly in the latter category; he worked on the line from 1887 until his retirement in 1921, and lived thereafter for many years in the Helston area. This record of service to the community certainly did not pass without notice, and in December 1937 the *Great Western Railway Magazine* printed the following paragraph:

> Living at Helston, in Cornwall, is Mr Sainthill Lindsey, who joined the West Cornwall Railway at Penzance in 1870. He was subsequently appointed foreman at St Ives, and in 1887 became passenger guard on the newly-opened Helston branch, where he remained until his retirement, in 1921, at the exceptional age of seventy-four. He is now in his ninety-first year, and although naturally a trifle frail he is in possession of all his faculties. He has a fund of interesting reminiscences of the half-a-century which he spent in the railway service, among them being in the great blizzard of March 1891, when his train was snowed up for about a week in the cutting between Nancegollan and Praze.

Staff employed at Helston in the British Railways period included (at various times) porters T.J. Thomas, Thompson, C. Uren and T.F. Pethick, checker R.D. Treloar and motor drivers A. Knowles, T. Hichens and S. Ibbetson.

Helston issued 36,006 tickets in 1903, the corresponding figures for 1913 and 1923 being 73,606 and 30,383 respectively. Thereafter, there was an apparent decline in the number of ordinary ticket sales, although the fact that around 100 season tickets were sold each year during the 1930s would indicate that many regular travellers preferred to pay for their journeys in this convenient way. In 1932 the station issued 16,215 ordinary tickets and 177 season tickets, while in 1938 10,558 ordinary tickets and 82 season tickets were issued.

In terms of goods traffic, Helston handled 7,894 tons of freight in 1903, rising to 12,995 tons in 1913 and 19,035 tons in 1923. In general, the station dealt with around 12,000 tons of freight per annum during the early 1930s, roughly half of this tonnage being in the form of inwards or outwards general merchandise traffic. In 1938, 17,029 tons were handled, including 9,526 tons of general merchandise and 4,445 tons of coal.

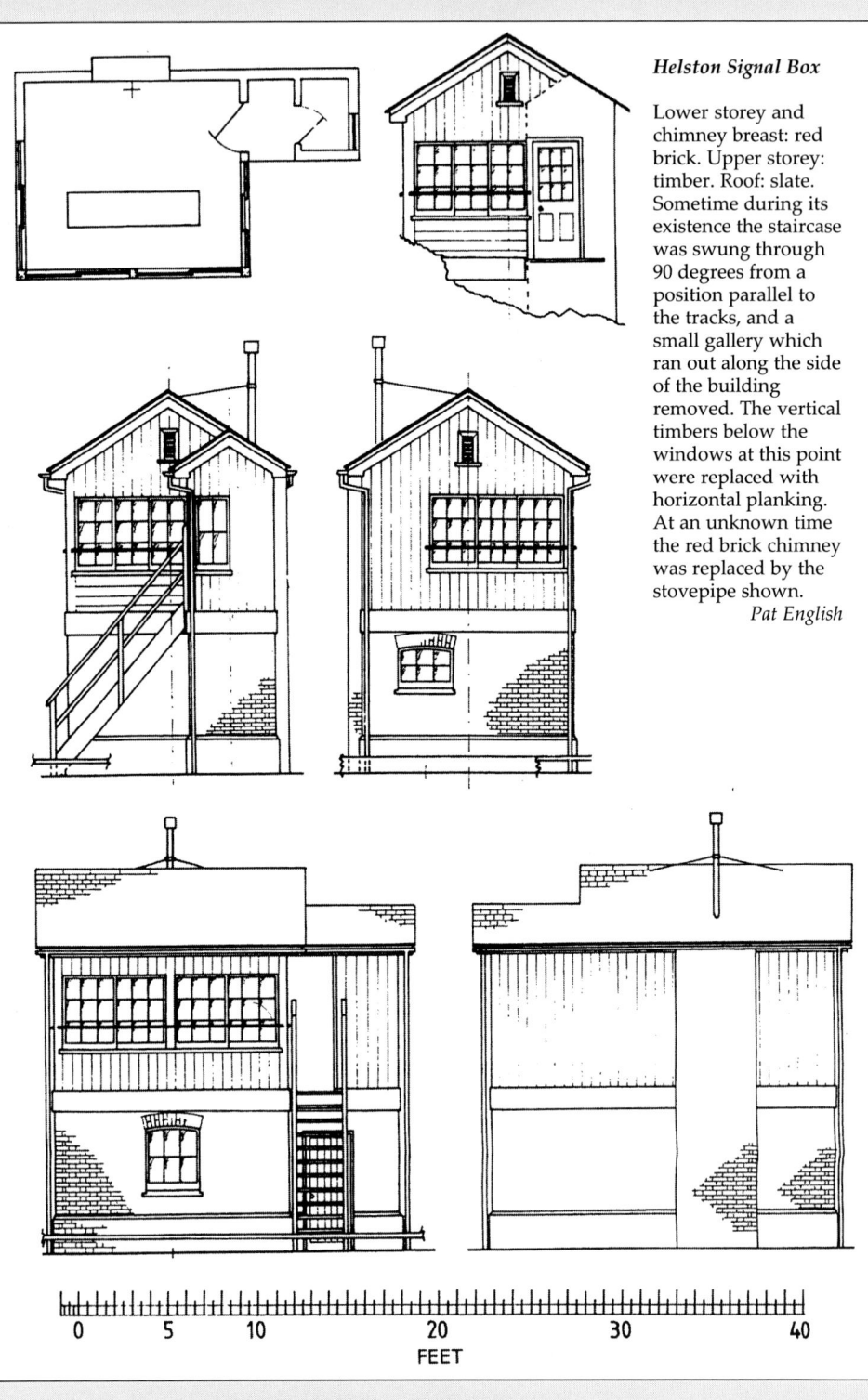

Helston Signal Box

Lower storey and chimney breast: red brick. Upper storey: timber. Roof: slate. Sometime during its existence the staircase was swung through 90 degrees from a position parallel to the tracks, and a small gallery which ran out along the side of the building removed. The vertical timbers below the windows at this point were replaced with horizontal planking. At an unknown time the red brick chimney was replaced by the stovepipe shown.

Pat English

The signal box at the north end of Helston platform had a lever frame with 11 signal levers, five point levers, two facing point levers and spaces for three spare levers. This rare interior view clearly shows the electric train staff instrument (*right*). *Oakwood Collection*

A detailed study of Helston signal box.
Pat English

A useful exterior view of the signal box, showing the porch at the Gwinear Road end of the signal box. *Philip J. Kelley Collection*

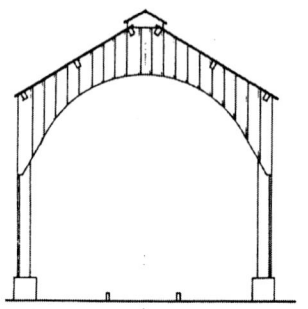
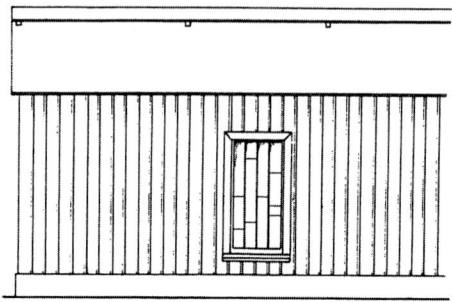
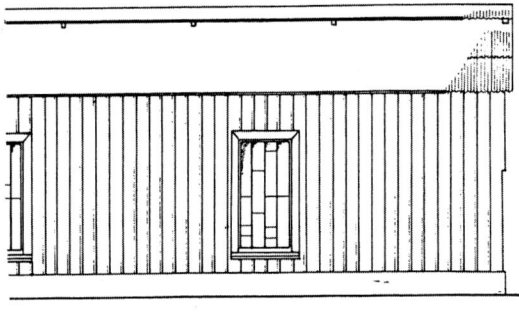
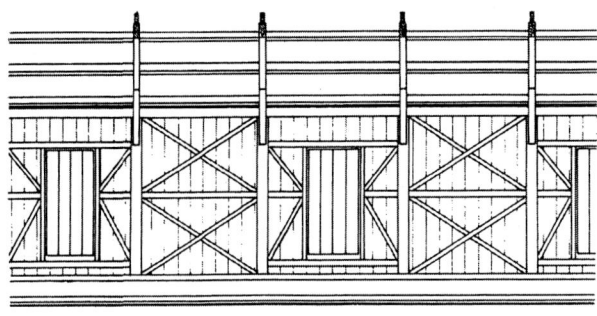

INSIDE DETAILS

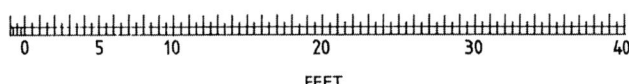

FEET

Helston Carriage Shed

Entirely timber-built and mounted on a cement rendered dwarf wall. The walls were clad with beaded vertical planking and the roof was of corrugated iron. *Pat English*

Above: Helston carriage shed from the east side. The joints between the vertical matchboarding were protected by thin laths or cover strips.

Left: The entrance to the carriage shed in May 1957. This wooden structure was situated at the very end of the line above the station approach road.

Below: A rare glimpse of the inside of Helston carriage shed, showing details of the internal framing and roof structure. *(All) Pat English*

Helston Goods Shed

Shed: all walls in natural stone; all corners, doors and windows faced in red brick; chimney in red brick; the walls above the rail openings were of beaded vertical planking; slate roof. Office: the wall facing the road elevation and its return to the main shed were in natural stone faced with red brick on the corners; the window in this wall was faced with white glazed brick; all other walls were cement render; slate roof. Office extension: walls were cement render with a flat tarred roof. By closure the sliding door shown on the drawing and fitted to the rail opening in the north-west end of the shed had been replaced by an internally-mounted 'up-and-over' segmented door. An early photograph shows that originally there was a small awning mounted over the cart opening to the shed.

Pat English

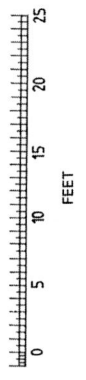
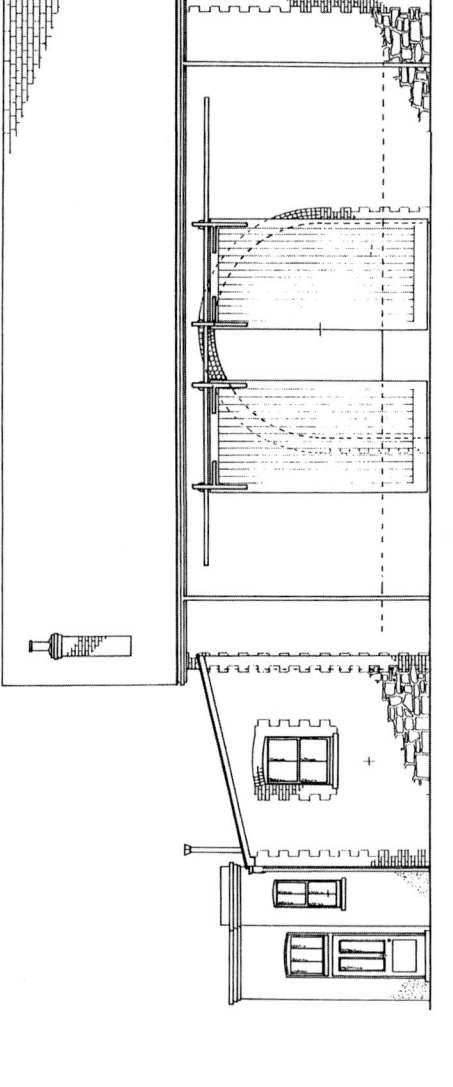

A roadside view of the goods shed at Helston station in May 1957.
Pat English

Two further views showing the southernmost extremity of the goods yard. The tumble-down wooden structure was a coal merchant's storage shed. *(Both) Pat English*

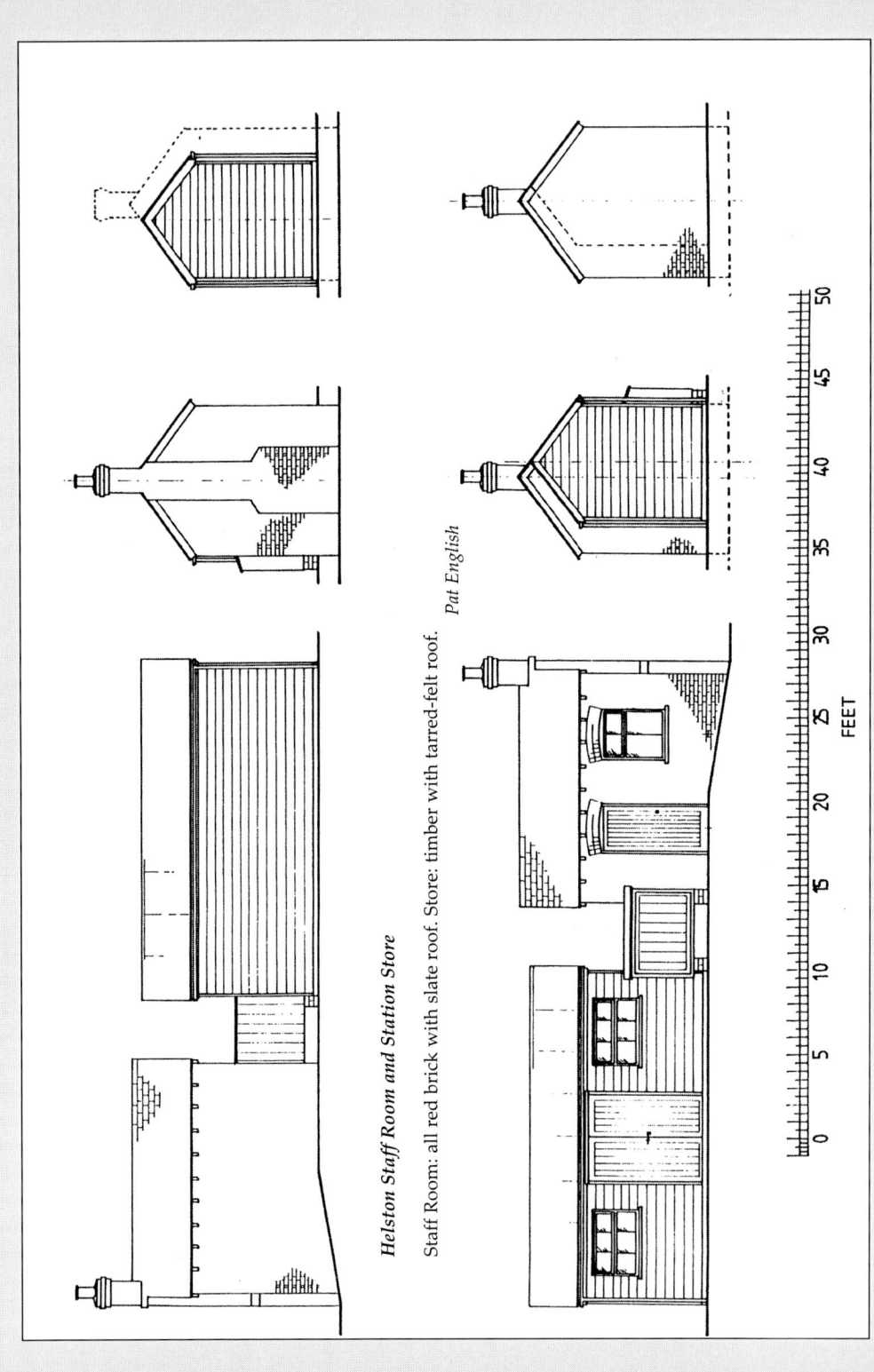

Helston Staff Room and Station Store

Staff Room: all red brick with slate roof. Store: timber with tarred-felt roof.

Pat English

The wooden storage shed at the north end of Helston station platform was about 20 ft long and 7 ft wide. *Pat English*

The adjacent, brick-built structure was used as a staff mess room in later years. It measured 13 ft 6 in. by 9 ft at ground level. It apparently started life as a 'foot warmer' house. *Pat English*

Traffic dealt with at Helston

Year	Staff	Receipts (£)	Tickets	Parcels	Goods tonnage
1903	11	16,642	36,006	22,566	7,894
1913	15	23,109	73,606	42,864	12,995
1923	14	38,930	30,383	47,005	19,035
1929	20	42,109	18,004	60,899	17,718
1935	22	32,599	13,013	67,606	11,732
1936	22	34,929	13,056	72,218	12,494
1937	22	35,565	12,720	72,323	15,972
1938	22	37,674	10,558	75,689	17,029

Helston itself was situated to the south, and south-west of the railway and, having left the station, visitors soon found themselves amid the plain, granite built houses of the old town; there was little of visible interest, and the writer of the 1903 *Little Guide to Cornwall* thought that Helston was 'not in reality, a very interesting place' - though it 'derived lustre from its old May-tide celebrations (8th May) known as Furry or Flora Day, when the inhabitants went out in the early morning to gather garlands and branches' and then danced through the streets to 'a kind of hornpipe, probably nearly as ancient as the celebration'.

The Furry Dance was, at one time, allowed to lapse, but it was revived during the late 19th century and soon became a tourist attraction. The GWR - only too glad to promote Cornish tourism - did much to publicize this old west country custom, and an article in the *Great Western Railway Magazine* described the event as follows:

> On May 8th the quaint old Cornish town of Helston hold its annual Furry dance. This is one of the most attractive old rights still observed in the West of England, and it naturally holds unusual appeal for tourists and strangers who happen to be in the district. Headed by the town band, many of the townsfolk dance in couples along the main street. A curious feature of this dance is that each couple may trip their way through the houses and cottages along the route, entering by the front door and passing out by the back, and vice versa. All doors are left open for the purpose.

Helston became something of a naval, town with the commissioning of the nearby naval air station at Culdrose on 17th April, 1947. In naval, parlance, this large shore establishment was regarded as a 'stone frigate' and, as such, it was dubbed HMS *Seahawk*; used initially as a naval air fighter school, RNAS Culdrose eventually became one of Britain's most important naval air stations - the movements of naval airmen being an important source of passenger traffic for the Helston branch prior to its closure in 1962.

Many naval families lived in Helston, the close links between Helston and the Navy being underlined by new housing estates with street names such as Hermes Road, Albion Road and Bulwark Road (named after post-war aircraft carriers), Bligh Crescent, Pellew Crescent and Esmonde Road (famous sailors) and Taranto Road. It was, perhaps, ironic that the Navy came to Helston, and brought extra traffic to its branch line, at a time when government policies were poised to do irreparable harm to the railway industry; within a few years, all movements of men or equipment to HMS *Seahawk* would, of necessity, be made by road transport - and the railway would be no more than a memory.

Chapter Five

Later History and Minor Details

The return of peace was followed by nationalization of the railways on 1st January, 1948, but this change of ownership produced few changes at Helston, and post-war train services were very similar to those provided during the 1930s. In 1949 for example, there were nine up and nine down workings, with extra trains on summer Saturdays. Post-war expansion of the Fleet Air Arm ensured that the Helston branch still carried large numbers of naval airmen en route to RNAS Culdrose, while in summertime the line was busy with holiday traffic.

Special trains were occasionally run in connection with personnel movements to or from the naval air station at Culdrose, and on such occasions two '45XX' class 2-6-2T locomotives could often be seen heading long trains of corridor coaches on the bucolic Helston route. At other times, aircraft components were delivered to Helston station by rail, bogie bolsters being used for the conveyance of aero-engines, propellers or other bulky items.

In locomotive terms, the British Railways era was somewhat disappointing as far as youthful 'spotters' were concerned, the vast majority of local train services being worked by the ubiquitous '45XX' class 2-6-2Ts that had worked on the line since the Great Western period. There was, on the other hand, a modicum of variety in that many individual engines appeared on the branch, typical numbers being: 4500, 4502, 4506, 4509, 4517, 4523, 4525, 4537, 4540, 4545, 4548, 4554, 4546, 4558, 4565, 4564, 4570, 4574, 4577 and 5562. Most of these 'Small Prairies' were of the earlier variety with 1,000 gallon capacity flat-topped tanks, but Nos. 4577 and 5562 had 1,500 gallon, sloping topped tanks. Three 2-6-2T locomotives were needed to work the normal branch train service, the usual practice being for one engine (often No. 4545) to be employed on passenger duties while two similar engines worked the freight turns.

'Dukedog' 4-4-0s were, as 'Yellow' engines, allowed to work on the Helston line, while '43XX' class 2-6-0s and '51XX' class 2-6-2Ts, in the heavier 'Blue' category, were permitted to work over the line subject to a 20 mph speed limit between 6 miles 40 chains and 8 miles 60 chains. These heavier engines are unlikely to have appeared on the route in peacetime, although it is conceivable that they may have hauled troop trains during World War II. Collett '58XX' class 0-4-2Ts were used on the line on a sporadic basis during the later GWR period, while '57XX' class pannier tanks are said to have been employed occasionally during the British Railways era.

Coaching stock consisted of standard Great Western two-coach, non-corridor 'B sets', though the usual rake was occasionally strengthened by the addition of one or more extra vehicles. The line was normally worked by two sets, which were designated 'Helston No.1' and 'Helston No. 2'. In the BR period, these two 'B sets' were formed of bow-ended brake composites Nos. 6445 + 6446, and 6461 + 6466 respectively. A former LMS suburban coach was noted on the branch in the immediate post-war era, albeit for a very short period.

On 14th April, 1960 '45XX' class 2-6-2T No. 4552 hurries along the branch between Praze and Gwinear Road. *P.Q. Treloar*

A late morning scene at Gwinear Road on 19th September, 1959. 'County' class 4-6-0 No. 1007 *County of Brecknock* pulls out of the down main line platform with a parcels and empty stock working, while '45XX' class 2-6-2T No. 4588 waits in the branch platform during a pause in shunting operations. *P.Q. Treloar*

LATER HISTORY AND MINOR DETAILS

'4575' class 2-6-2T No. 4588 heads a mixed freight formation along the Helston branch.
P.Q. Treloar

'4575' class 2-6-2T No. 4577 heads a pick-up freight along the branch.
P.Q. Treloar

'45XX' class 2-6-2T No. 4570 with the six-coach 1.19 pm service, shortly after leaving Helston on Saturday 30th August, 1958. *P.Q. Treloar*

The 1.15 pm from Helston to Gwinear Road climbs towards the Cober viaduct on 30th August, 1958. No. 4570 heads a strengthened six-coach formation. *P.Q. Treloar*

Collett '45XX' class 2-6-2T No. 4571 heads a Helston branch train.
P.Q. Treloar

Collett '4575' class 2-6-2T No. 5541 stands in the branch platform at Gwinear Road.
P.Q. Treloar

A passenger train at Nancegollan, photographed from the road overbridge. *P.Q. Treloar*

'45XX' class 2-6-2T No. 4565 leaves Nancegollan with a down train. *P.Q. Treloar*

LATER HISTORY AND MINOR DETAILS

'45XX' class 2-6-2T No. 4571 stands in the down platform at Nancegollan with the 2.20 pm from Gwinear Road to Helston on 14th April, 1960. The bridge in the background was extended when the station was rebuilt during the 1930s, the left-hand (girder) span being a later addition while the arched stone span was originally built by the Helston Railway. *P.Q. Treloar*

Up and down trains in the crossing loop at Nancegollan. *P.Q. Treloar*

Road competition

The return to peacetime conditions in 1945, and the subsequent removal of petrol rationing and other restrictions, soon led to a rapid change in the pattern of local transport. The private motor car really came into its own, changing completely the travelling habits of a large number of people. There was, as a result, no longer the same reliance upon rail travel - either for business or for leisure purposes; at the same time, long distance coach services were improving, while internal air services began to complete with the railway for long distance travel.

The railways experienced similar cut-throat competition on the freight side; in this case, the rapid reorganization of industry, changes in marketing methods, and the demand for quick transit with minimal handling contributed to a rapid expansion of road haulage. With the nationalization of road transport during the immediate post-war period, there were hopes that real co-ordination and integration of road and rail transport would take place but, with a change of government in 1953, came an abrupt change of policy which led to the denationalisation of road (but not rail) transport. This upset the whole balance of the nation's transport policy, bringing more and more motor vehicles onto the roads and causing the loss of more and more vulnerable rail traffic.

Government policies thereby contributed to an approaching crisis on the railways. The steam age, having served its purpose for over a century, was giving way, somewhat reluctantly, to new ideas in transport. The railways were confronted with ever-growing competition and, in spite of great efforts to make the system viable, the British Railways network faced heavier and heavier costs.

On a happier note, a small ceremony was held at Helston station on 17th August, 1953 to mark the 50th anniversary of the introduction of road motor services to and from the Lizard. The ceremony was attended by several former employees, and also the Mayor of Helston, who unveiled a small commemorative plaque recalling the 'first railway motor omnibus service, which was run by the Great Western Railway from Helston to the Lizard on 17th August 1903'.

Towards Closure

In retrospect, it is now clear that the 1950s were an Indian summer for rural lines such as the Helston branch. Government policies and rival forms of transport were insidiously conspiring to undermine the very existence of such lines, although this was by no means clear at the time. Many people expected the national railway system to be maintained in its entirety as a vital part of the nation's infrastructure, and the Helston branch - which still carried a significant amount of holiday traffic -seemed to have a fairly secure future ahead of it.

Fares were, in the middle-1950s, still remarkably cheap, and it is staggering to consider that, in 1960, the ordinary return fare from Paddington to Helston was only 112 shillings. The corresponding return fares from a range of other towns and cities were as follows:

Bath Spa	to	Helston	82s. 0d.
Manchester London Road	"	"	136s. 0d.
Kidderminster	"	"	106s. 0d.
Wolverhampton Low Level	"	"	114s. 0d.
Birmingham Snow Hill	"	"	110s. 0d.
Oxford	"	"	104s. 0d.
Plymouth	"	"	29s. 6d.
Reading	"	"	100s. 0d.
Leeds City	"	"	148s. 0d.

Single fares were usually half the return fares, while first class tickets were available at prices around 50 per cent above the ordinary second class fares. For enthusiasts, walkers, or other active holidaymakers, BR also offered a good-value 'Runabout' season ticket covering an area bounded by Penzance, St Ives, Helston, Perranporth, Truro, Falmouth, St Austell, Par, Roche and Newquay; this cost just 18s. 6d. for seven days unlimited travel, throughout west Cornwall while, for the slightly higher price of 24s. 6d., one could also include travel on the River Fal between Falmouth and Truro.

Dieselization in Cornwall

One small change initiated under British Railways auspices was the introduction of diesel traction on Cornish branch lines such as the Helston route. Although dieselization had commenced in East Anglia (and other areas) at a slightly earlier date, there was an important distinction between the policies adopted in the West Country and elsewhere. In general, BR local services were entrusted to diesel multiple units, but in Devon and Cornwall the tendency was for local freight and passenger workings to be hauled by diesel locomotives. For this purpose the Western Region introduced a class of 58 Bo-Bo locomotives, which were originally known as the North British Locomotive Company type '2s'. Of 1,100 horse power (the first six were of 1,000 hp), they were numbered in the D63XX series from 6300 to 6357. Like other Western Region diesel locomotives they were diesel-hydraulics rather than diesel-electrics, and they were further distinguished by having spoked wheels (an unusual feature on diesel locomotives).

The NBL type '2s' were first introduced in 1959, and the first members of the class were soon hard at work on Cornish branches, the Helston line becoming one of their strongholds. Like all Western Region diesel locomotives, the North British diesel-hydraulics (which later became known as class '22s') were classified in the Great Western route availability system, and Nos. D6306-57 were designated 'Yellow' engines. As such, they were suitable for use on the Helston route as replacements for the '45XX' class 2-6-2Ts, and the NBL type '2s' were well-established on the line by 1962. Sadly, these modern locomotives were introduced at a time when the future of the Helston branch was in the balance, and in the event the diesel era at Helston was destined of be of very short duration.

A gathering of Western Region transport officials with the Mayor and other council dignitaries on 17th August, 1953, pose in front of the plaque commemorating the first motor bus services run by the GWR. *Philip J. Kelley Collection*

A close-up of the plaque on the day that it was unveiled. *Philip J. Kelley Collection*

The Beeching period

A plan for reorganization, streamlining and modernization of British Railways, produced under Sir Brian Robertson's Chairmanship of the British Transport Commission, was inherited by his successor, Dr Richard Beeching, who commenced work on a controversial reshaping scheme - now known as the Beeching Plan.

Basing his conclusions on an exceedingly narrow financial model, Beeching concluded that much of Britain's railway system was 'uneconomic', and he therefore recommended the withdrawal of passenger services from 5,000 miles of line, together with the closure of over 2,500 stations. Duplicate routes would be eliminated, and what freight traffic then remained would be concentrated in a limited number of major centres. As far as Cornwall was concerned, the Beeching proposals (when published in March 1963) envisaged the closure of most local branch lines, and the withdrawal of most stopping services on the former GWR main line.

In a logical move towards the implementation of the Beeching plan, the Helston branch became the first in Cornwall to lose its passenger services since the 1930s. Late in 1961, rumours of impending closure began to circulate; meetings were held and protests were made by town and rural district councils, by chambers of commerce, by the National Farmers Union, and many other bodies. Members of Parliament made representations to the Minister of Transport, and a strong case was put before the Transport Users' Consultative Committee; in fact, everything which could be done, was done in an effort to reprieve the line, but all efforts were of no avail.

The stark fact was that the local railway had been overtaken by the march of events; the amount of passenger traffic needed to make the branch viable no longer passed by rail, and the Minister of Transport, after full consideration of all the facts, confirmed that the line would be closed to passenger traffic with effect from 5th November, 1962. As this was a Monday, the last trains would run on Saturday 3rd November, 1962. Truthall Halt would be closed completely, but Praze, Nancegollan and Helston stations would remain open for freight and parcels traffic.

The withdrawal of passenger services

The *West Briton and Cornwall Advertiser*, which had fully reported the cutting of the sod ceremony on 22nd March, 1882 and the opening ceremony of the Helston Railway on 9th May, 1887, reported again, (this time as the *West Briton & Royal Cornwall Gazette*) the closing scenes of the Helston branch passenger services on 3rd November, 1962. This sad occasion saw the largest gathering of people for many years at Helston station. All through the day many called to purchase tickets as souvenirs and take a last look at the little branch line which had been overwhelmed by events, and was now performing its last function as a link with the outside world.

The doomed branch line was busy throughout the day, and in order to cater for the many extra travellers BR strengthened the 4.10 pm up service to four coaches. As evening approached, the crowds thinned out slightly, but many people later

The last train from Helston arrives at Gwinear Road behind class '22' Bo-Bo No. D6312 on the evening of Saturday 3rd November, 1962. *Pat English*

Anti-closure demonstrators (one carrying a symbolic 'axe') throng the darkened platforms at Gwinear Road on 3rd November, 1962. *Pat English*

made their way to the stations at Helston, Nancegollan and Praze in order to see the very last scheduled passenger service, and well over 150 sightseers were on the platform at Helston when the last train drew out at 8.45 pm.

This final up working consisted of six non-corridor coaches, and over 120 people were aboard as the train commenced its melancholy journey to Gwinear Road. This last scheduled up service was hauled by NBL type '2' diesel locomotive No. D6312, and driven by Mr J. Ellis of St Ives, with Mr A. Rowe as second man and Mr W.M. Evans in charge as guard. A group of young men dressed as mourners travelled on the train to Gwinear Road and back, while large numbers of people had, by this time, assembled at Nancegollan and Gwinear Road stations to witness the closing of the line to passenger traffic. After making its connection with a main line working (the 2.30 pm down service from Paddington) the last southbound branch train departed from Gwinear Road to the singing of *Auld Lang Syne* which was again heard as the train was leaving Nancegollan.

The train arrived back at Helston by 9.59 pm, some 10 minutes late owing to the 'last rites' activities that had been taking place at the intermediate stations; fireworks were let off, detonators exploded, and photographs were taken; tape recordings were made, and a few people were permitted to ride on the engine but, in spite of some hilarity, there was a deep feeling, especially among the older people, that those present were witnessing the closing of an era. It was a sad ending.

The engine bore a large wreath from 'Old Helstonian Grammar School Train Boys', many of whom had been regular travellers in by-gone days, and some of whom had made the journey on this last occasion. The grammar school (the early history of which remains unknown) existed long before the year 1610, when the school was rebuilt, and it thus had a long association with the town. The headmaster in 1882 was Mr J.W. Savery, who was present at the cutting of the turf ceremony on 22nd March of that year. During the years which followed, many pupils from the Nancegollan and Praze areas travelled to and from Helston by train, and it was fitting that so many were present on the occasion of the last run, thus maintaining an interest in the railway right up to its end.

So far as the members of the public were concerned the arrival of the last train at Helston marked the closing of the line, but for the staff, 'closing time' had not yet arrived, as they were still busy with the disposal of the empty stock of the train. The signalman, who had restored signal lever No. 1, the down main home, to 'danger' immediately the incoming train had passed it, collected the train staff from the engineman, restored it to the instrument, and sent the 'train out of section' signal to his colleague at Nancegollan. The engine, which in the meantime had been uncoupled, then ran round its train via the engine loop and main line, and was recoupled to the empty stock, after which the tail lamp of the train was reversed. The signalman then sent the 'call attention' signal to Nancegollan and on receiving an acknowledgement asked 'is line clear?' for an empty stock train, withdrew the staff from the instrument, gave it to the engineman, lowered his up main starting and up main advanced starting signals. After the guard had given the right away to the engineman and the train had started, the 'train entering section' signal was sent to Nancegollan. The time was 10.14 pm, and this was duly recorded in the train register.

Having reached Helston on the last train, a number of railway enthusiasts from Plymouth and other 'up country' destinations found themselves stranded at the terminus, but a request for permission to travel back to Gwinear Road on the empty coaches was refused by the guard on the grounds that, if passengers boarded the train, it would no longer be an 'empty stock working'. After the train of empty coaches had cleared Nancegollan, and the Helston signalman had received the 'train out of section' signal from Nancegollan, he completed his record in the train register, signed off duty, closed the signal box and left the station. In the meantime, a considerable traffic jam had built-up in the station approach road as Western National buses and the large numbers of private cars that had been parked at the station attempted to leave at the same time.

The post-closure period

The cessation of passenger services did not affect the still-busy freight service between Helston and Gwinear Road, and the line was retained in being for a further two years as a freight-only route. Local enthusiasts hoped that the route would remain in being for many years but, sadly, the Beeching programme saw no place for small freight or sundries traffic such as that handled at Helston, and at a time when small goods stations were being ruthlessly closed throughout the country, it was clear that, even as a goods-only line, the Helston branch had no long term future. The axe eventually fell on 4th October, 1964, on which day the Helston branch was officially closed to all traffic.

No time was lost in taking up the rails; demolition work started in the early months of 1965, and the entire line had been dismantled by the end of the year. With the removal of the last rail, the end of the line was finally reached, and Helston people realised that, as far as their town was concerned, the railway age was well and truly finished.

The former station at Helston was used for a time by the Western National Omnibus Co., but otherwise the place was silent and forlorn; the site was later redeveloped. Praze and Nancegollan stations, meanwhile, were demolished, though the road overbridge at Nancegollan station remained as a gaunt reminder of happier days. Traces of platforms and other features could still be seen, while bridges and earthworks survived at various places along the line as monuments to the abandoned railway.

Gwinear Road station remained open after the 1962 branch closure, but this respite was only temporary, and the erstwhile junction station was deleted from the national railway system with effect from 5th October 1964. Goods facilities remained in use at Gwinear Road for a few more months, but the end finally came in August 1965, with the closure of Gwinear Road East and Gwinear Road West signal boxes, all remaining sidings and connections at the former junction station being taken out of use at that time. Meanwhile, the famous level crossing gates were taken down, and in their place BR erected efficient, but somewhat characterless, automatic lifting half-barriers. Otherwise, very little remained of the once-busy junction where, in days gone by, travellers had changed into a two-coach branch train for the 8¾ mile journey to Helston.

LATER HISTORY AND MINOR DETAILS

Conclusion

The history of the Helston branch is, in many ways, the history of Britain's railways in general. Built at a time of unbounded business confidence by an imperial nation at the very height of its power, the railway rapidly became outmoded when rival forms of transport were developed in the 20th century. The Helston line nevertheless continued to serve the community as a public service for many more years, and in World War II it became of vital importance. However, the branch then became a victim of politics when the government of the day (urged on by permanent civil servants in the Ministry of Transport) decided that railways were of less value than roads. In advanced industrialized countries such as France or Germany, a line such as the Helston route would have been retained, and indeed modernized, as part of the vital infrastructure of a modern state, but post-Imperial Britain, locked into a spiral of decline, could offer only cuts and retraction in the face of endless economic difficulties. In these circumstances, it was perhaps inevitable that the Helston line (never a spectacularly successful route in terms of economics) should have become an early victim of the government's axe.

The Helston branch has, therefore, passed into history, but the line is still fresh in many people's memories, and there are several relics of the railway in Helston and the surrounding area. At Helston, for example, the distinctive goods shed has been the subject of an interesting domestic conversion; now standing in the middle of a modern housing development, this substantial stone-built structure could easily be mistaken for an old non-conformist chapel, but closer examination reveals the position of the large end doors through which railway goods vehicles once entered the building.

The Cober viaduct at Lowertown still spans Rocky Valley; its preservation would form a fitting and perpetual memorial to the little branch line, which originated as the 'Helston Railway'.

The Helston Folk Museum contains many relics of the erstwhile Helston Railway, including the silver wheelbarrow used at the sod-cutting ceremony on 22nd March, 1882, a debenture register, a programme of events for the sod-cutting, menu cards and photographs of the decorated arches erected in connection with the 1882 festivities. There are also photographs of the Mayor and corporation, Directors and other, taken outside the station on the opening day on 9th May 1887, together with photographs of the station, the railway-owned motor buses, and long-serving Helston branch guard Sainthill Lindsey in his GWR guard's uniform. In another part of the museum, the bearded, patriarchal face of William Bickford-Smith stares impassively from his framed portrait, while related displays deal with fishing, mining and other aspects of the local economy during the 19th century. Much of this material provides background information in relation to the Helston Railway and its promoters.

The original seal of the Helston Railway, a fine specimen showing the borough arms with St Michael slaying the dragon, is now in the Railway Museum at Swindon.

Envoi

Gone forever are the days when passengers for Helston looked forward to arriving at Gwinear Road, changing into the branch train, and spending the last 25 minutes of their train journey travelling through Praze, with its lovely wood by Clowance wall, Nancegollan, on to Truthall Platform so lonely and isolated, then over the deep rocky valley, spanned by the Cober viaduct, and on to Helston.

Those who made that journey on so many occasions, some happy, some sad, would never again be able to look out of the train for a first glimpse of Helston station platform - and perhaps of someone awaiting their arrival. There was no experience quite equal to that of arriving 'home' at a small branch line station. There were, first of all, greetings to be exchanged with the guard, engineman and fireman of the branch train while awaiting departure from the main line station; at your destination you might be spotted by some of the older members of the staff, who had known you for years, and would greet you with a warmth that was genuine and sincere.

The age of steam is past; the branch line has closed, and many will think nostalgically, and perhaps with affection, of the link which bound Helston with the rest of the county, and with England, and of the part it played in the lives of its people, not only at its inception, but throughout the 75 years of its existence.

Trackwork

It would, finally be useful to say a few words about trackwork, tickets and certain other minor details that cannot easily be filled into a coherent narrative. The next two sections (and the appendices which follow) will therefore include a few miscellaneous details appertaining to the Helston branch.

Colonel Rich's 1887 inspection report reveals that the Helston Railway was originally laid with 70 lb. per yard flat-bottomed rail, attached to ordinary wooden cross sleepers. Although several other GWR branches built at the end of the 19th century, including the Staines West and Tetbury lines, were laid with flat-bottomed rail, this type of trackwork was castigated as contractor's or 'Yankee' rail during the Victorian period, and the branch was soon re-laid with conventional bullhead rail resting in cast-iron chairs. Photographs show that the earlier flat-bottomed track was retained, for a few years, in goods yards and sidings – one of the last sections of flat-bottomed rail being at Helston, where the stone chute siding seems to have been laid with such rail during the 1920s.

Helston railway minutes contain odd references to the need for 'double flanging' on some of the sharp curves between Helston and Gwinear Road, and photographic evidence shows that double flanges (i.e. check rails) had been installed by the 1890s; a well-known photograph taken at Helston around 1900 shows that the sharp curve on the approach to the terminus had been check-railed by that date.

The line retained its bullhead-pattern trackwork until the BR era, and apart from the routine replacement of time-expired equipment, there were few changes prior to closure. The line was, in general, always laid with wooden cross sleepers, though some concrete sleepers were installed during the last few years of operation.

LATER HISTORY AND MINOR DETAILS

A note on tickets

As far as can be ascertained the tickets issued at Praze, Nancegollan and Helston stations were always of standard Great Western design, though it is possible that some early issues may have been distinguished, by the legend 'Helston Ry.' There was, initially, an astounding range of bookings, and until World War I each GWR ticket was printed in a variety of differing colours; dog tickets, for example, were multi-coloured red, buff and blue issues, while 'government rate' tickets for military personnel were printed on green cards with a broad yellowish-buff horizontal stripe. The vast majority of tickets held at Helston and the other stations were standard-sized Edmondson card tickets, measuring 57 mm by 30 mm. They carried the names of issuing stations and destinations, together with fares, class designations and other data.

The complex colour-coded system used by the GWR prior to World War I had been much simplified by the 1930s, but there were still many different types of booking, each being distinguished by a strict colour system. First class tickets from Helston to Gwinear Road, for instance, were white, while corresponding third class issues were printed on green cards. Other distinguishing colours in use during the 1930s were as follows: children's' tickets - blue; workmen's tickets - grey or pink; third class excursions - yellowish buff; bicycle tickets - brown; perambulators - pink; government rate tickets - green; dog tickets - dark red.

The tickets were further distinguished, in the case of return issues, by the addition of 'skeleton letters' which were superimposed on the return half to denote the type of booking. Some typical examples are shown below:

R	Ordinary return	L	Long period return
C	Cheap day return	TD	Theatrical performer
CD	Circular day trip	PC	Poor children
CT	Commercial traveller	TS	Training ship boy
GR	Government rate	BI	Bicycle
O	Officer on leave	PP	Privilege ticket
D	Dog ticket	PN	Picnic party
A	American	WE	Weekend
AN	Angler	E	Excursion
W	Waiters	F	Fishworker
T	Tourist		

Road motor tickets issued in connection with the Lizard bus service were originally printed on Edmondson cards, but vertical, bus-type tickets were introduced at an early date.

Great Western tickets remained in use for several years after nationalization but, as stocks became exhausted, Helston and the other stations received new, BR tickets. These were generally similar to those used during the Great Western period, in that first class issues were printed on white Edmondson cards, workmen's tickets were still grey, and excursion tickets continued to be printed on buff cards. Small changes included the abolition of third class bookings and the introduction of second class facilities - BR second class tickets being printed

Bagnall 0-4-0ST *Judy* on the weekend of the formal opening of Trevarno station on 24th/25th July, 2010. This locomotive was made available with the kind permission of the Bodmin & Wenford Railway for that weekend only and is not based on the Helston Railway. In the background is one of the Ruston & Hornsby diesel shunters. *Stuart Walker*

The Park Royal class '103' two-car multiple unit in the platform at Trevarno bears the name 'Helston' on its destination blind. *Stuart Walker*

on light green cards. Bicycle tickets changed from brown to red during the BR period, while the blue children's tickets were abolished; instead, travellers under 14 were issued with ordinary white (first) or green (second class) tickets, distinguished by bright red 'CHILD' overprints.

Another change introduced under BR auspices was the introduction of red overprints instead of the less conspicuous 'skeleton' letters favoured by the GWR - a British Railways second class return ticket from Praze to Helston would thus have been a light green Edmondson card bearing a large red 'R' on its return half. To take just one more example, a cheap day return, say from Penzance to Helston, would have been printed on buff card with a red 'D' on its return portion.

The study of tickets is a fascinating aspect of local railway history, and surviving 'Edmondsons' are today changing hands at surprisingly high prices. These small, coloured pieces of card are interesting reminders of vanished railways such as the Helston branch, and it is interesting to reflect that, in years to come, tickets issued at Praze, Nancegollan and Helston will still be lovingly preserved in private collections, long after the railway has ceased to exist.

Revival at Trevarno

Although a scheme to reopen the Helston branch during the 1980s did not come to fruition, a subsequent proposal that was put forward in conjunction with the Trevarno Estate in 2005 has met with considerably more success. The revived 'Helston Railway' is located on the guided walk that encircles the idyllic gardens, and this ensures that it will be encountered by most visitors - including many who are not 'conventional' railway enthusiasts. The Helston Railway Preservation Company Limited is a 'social enterprise' company limited by guarantee, its aim being the re-opening of a section of the former Helston Branch Line. The company is run on a 'not for profit' basis, and any excess of income over expenditure is re-invested into the railway.

Trevarno, which is now the centre of operations on this revived section of the Helston Railway, consists of a through platform and terminal bay, which is sited beside the stone-arched road overbridge, together with one connected siding and a detached spur. The platform is constructed from old timber sleepers, while the edging stones were obtained from Penryn when the passing loop was installed on the Falmouth branch. A 'GUV' van that has been positioned on the detached spur serves as a museum and shop. Future plans include the provision of a run-round loop and a siding, which will be laid between the station and Tregadjack Farm overbridge.

A plate girder footbridge has been erected immediately to the south of the station to carry a public footpath over the proposed Truthall extension, and although this is a brand new structure, its design was inspired by the similar bridge that once stood at Nancegollan station.

About half a mile of trackwork has been laid northwards from Trevarno towards Gansey Farm, using second-hand concrete sleepers and rail from the Falmouth branch. Much of the ballast in use is the original, supplemented by some material from the Falmouth branch; some of the track was laid by naval parties from RNAS Culdrose.

At the time of writing, there are plans to re-lay a further half mile of track in a southerly direction between Trevarno and Truthall Halt. The tangled undergrowth has been cleared from this section by Helston Railway volunteers - the vegetation being almost jungle-like, with a mixture of gorse, bramble bushes and rhododendrons, while farmers had filled-in some of the cuttings. It is envisaged that Truthall Halt will be re-instated and, although the branch was single track, the formation widens sufficiently at Truthall to allow the installation of a run-round loop.

The locomotives and rolling available for use in 2010 included two Ruston & Hornsby 0-4-0 diesel shunters, a Park Royal class '103' two-car multiple unit, a BR standard brake van and the GUV. The Rustons are both former industrial shunters, one of which (works No. 327974) was used by the British Sugar Corporation, while its companion (works No. 395305) worked for ICI at Runcorn and, later, at Smalldale Quarry in Derbyshire. The class '103' set, comprising motor brake second No. 50413 and driving trailer composite No. 56169 is not yet operational, although one of its engines has been started. It is likely that the initial train services will be worked, push-pull fashion, by a diesel shunter and one of the class '103' vehicles.

It is conceivable that, like other 'heritage' lines, the Helston Railway could attract visiting steam locomotives - a precedent having been set on 24th-25th July, 2010 when the Bodmin & Wenford Railway's 'cut-down' 0-4-0ST Bagnall 0-4-0ST *Judy* was loaned to the Helston Railway in connection with the formal opening of Trevarno station.

Volunteers hard at work ballasting a point on the Helston Railway. *Stuart Walker*

Appendix One

Some Locomotives used on the Helston Branch

Class	Type	Typical Nos.
Churchward prototype	0-4-4T	34/55
'517' class	0-4-2T	69/1158/1163/1481
'Metro'	2-4-0T	1496/3582
Churchward '44XX'	2-6-2T	4401/4403/4405/4406/4408/4409
Churchward '45XX'	2-6-2T	4500/4509/4517/4523/4525/4537/4540/4545/4548/ 4554/4558/4563/4564/4570/4574/4577
'2021' class	0-6-0ST	2097/2148
'850' class	0-6-0ST	859/992/1935/1943/1973/1989/2019
'58XX' class	0-4-2T	5812
'2700' class	0-6-0ST	2752
'North British Type '2'	Bo-Bo	D6308/D6309/D6312

'45XX' class 2-6-2T No. 4570 on the level crossing at Gwinear Road while engaged in running round its train. As no branch line loop was available this took place via the down main line. *Pat English*

Appendix Two

Chronology of Important Dates

1819	Proposed tramway from Hayle to Helston.
1825	Proposed tramways from Redruth to Penryn and Helston.
1834	Suggested lines from Redruth to Portreath and Helston.
1837	Opening of Hayle Railway (23rd December).
1846	Proposed railway from Penryn to Helston.
1852	West Cornwall Railway opens station at Gwinear Road.
1864	Helston & Penryn Junction Railway scheme receives Royal Assent (14th July).
1872	New plans for line from Penryn to Helston.
1879	Helston Railway formed by local landowners.
1880	Helston Railway Bill read for the 1st and 2nd time (10th February).
	Helston Railway Bill receives the Royal Assent (9th July).
1882	First sod cut at Helston (22nd March).
	Operating agreement with GWR (5th April).
1883	Works suspended.
1886	Work under way with new contractors (Messrs Lang & Son of Liskeard).
1887	Completed line inspected by Board of Trade (6th May).
	Helston Railway opened for public traffic (9th May).
1891	Line blocked by snow after the 'great blizzard' (March).
1892	West Cornwall main line converted to standard gauge.
1898	Helston Railway amalgamated with GWR (1st July).
1903	First GWR motor bus service introduced from Helston to the Lizard (August),
1904	GWR motor buses Nos. 3 and 8 destroyed by fire at Helston (29th September).
1905	Lizard bus service resumed following dispute with council (10th April).
	New halt opened at Truthall (3rd July).
1906	Truthall Halt becomes Truthall Platform (July).
1908	Intermediate crossing place opened at Nancegollan Loop.
1909	GWR motor bus service introduced between Helston and Porthleven.
1915	Helston station track layout altered (May).
1928	The railways obtain powers to operate road transport services.
1929	Helston bus services relinquished by the GWR (1st January).
1933	Last GWR bus handed over to associated bus company (31st December).
1937	Second platform, new buildings and other improvements at Nancegollan.
	New 20 ton weigh-bridge installed at Helston for motor lorries.
1938	Minor improvements at Gwinear Road station.
1939	Start of World War II (3rd September) - branch train services reduced.
1940	Branch patrolled by armoured train during wartime invasion scare.
	Construction work begins on Predannack airfield.
1944	Work begins on RNAS Culdrose - airfield construction traffic on railway.
1947	Commissioning of RNAS Culdrose (17th April).
1948	Nationalization of railways (1st January).
1956	Improved stone-handling facilities installed at Helston.
1958	Minor re-signalling arrangements put into effect at Helston station.
1962	Dieselization of branch train services (summer timetable).
	Helston branch closed to passenger traffic (Saturday 3rd November).
1964	Helston branch closed to all traffic.
1965	Demolition of Helston branch.
2010	Opening of Trevarno station.

Appendix Three

Station Facilities

Although details of each station have been given in Chapter Four, it may be worth describing the infrastructure of the Helston branch, in a more formalized way, and the following section has therefore been included in the hope that it may be of use to modellers (or others) seeking factual information about each station. Unless otherwise stated, the details given relate to the late GWR and early BR period around 1945-1955.

Gwinear Road

Up and down platforms for main line traffic
Branch platform for Helston line
Wooden station building on down (island) platform and brick building on up side
Steel girder pedestrian footbridge
East and West signal boxes
Two sidings plus loading bank on west side of station (up side)
Up and down goods refuge lines (loop on up side & sidings on down)
Six-road yard on down side of station
Cattle dock and associated spur (down side)
Weigh-house, lamp hut and permanent way hut, etc.

Praze

Single passenger platform on up side
Brick-built booking office/waiting rooms/toilets (approx. 60½ ft by 15½ ft)
Single goods siding
Single-storey lever cabin
Weigh-house
'Mushroom' (i.e. pedestal) water tank with flexible delivery hose
Permanent way hut/store

Nancegollan

Up and down platforms
Brick-built booking office/waiting rooms/parcels office/toilets (62 ft by 15 ft)
Six-road goods yard
Goods shed and extensive loading bank plus cattle pens
Standard GWR signal cabin (approx. 20 feet by 12 feet)
Waiting shelter on up platform
Weigh-house, permanent way hut, etc
Camping coach

Truthall Halt

Single platform on down side
Corrugated iron 'pagoda' shelter (approx. 20 ft by 8 ft)

Helston

Single passenger platform on up side
Run-round loop
Loop siding plus dead-end extension ('mileage' siding)
'Back' or loading bank siding
Stone chute spur
Stone-built booking office/waiting room/toilets/parcels office (approx 100 ft by 25 ft)
Standard GW signal cabin with 21 lever frame (including spares)
Stone goods shed
Stone-built locomotive shed and associated spur (shed 43 ft by 21 ft)
Wooden carriage shed (approx. 100 ft by 15 ft)
Road motor shed
Cattle loading pens
Weigh-house, lamp hut, etc
'Mushroom' water tank with flexible hose
Porters mess room (approx.13½ ft by 9 ft)
Store shed (20 ft by 7 ft)
Two locomotive coaling bunkers (2) and ash bunker
Six-ton fixed yard crane
Permanent way hut

Helston station, looking north towards Gwinear Road. *Lens of Sutton Collection*

Appendix Four

Helston in 3 mm Scale
by Keith Gowen

I have often been asked why I undertook such a project and how I started, a difficult question to answer but hopefully in these pages I can share with the reader some thoughts on how I re-created Helston in a scale of 3 mm to one foot.

Model railway enthusiasts, once they have overcome trying to collect or model a whole railway company's network, will, if they are to take up the hobby seriously, start to specialize in exactly the same way as a philatelist. They will look for an area that interests them, which includes their favourite locomotives and gradually zoom into a station layout that can be adjusted to suit their accommodation or perhaps more importantly, their ability to model their desired location. This will be a challenge and may be easy because of research already undertaken by an author of a book on that particular railway, or they may have to start with very little.

I started by purchasing six photographs produced by OPC a few years earlier when that challenge previously mentioned, took a grip. My attention was drawn to a series of articles by Pat English in the *Model Railway News* which further whetted the appetite.

First thoughts were that the layout would be built to exhibition standards - therefore it must be transportable, thus size had to be considered. A very good colleague, Geoff Gamble, supplied me with further photographs, together with a copy of Oakwood Press's earlier production on the line. However, when I started to piece the information together I was missing a plan of the signal box. Also no clear information existed on buildings beyond the goods shed, except that a carriage shed was resident on the through line at the buffer stops.

At this time a stroke of luck occurred whilst I was trying to contact the Helston Museum. I unexpectedly came into contact with an Helstonian railway enthusiast who had access to plans of the station. These plans enabled me to calculate the floor area of the signal box and with the use of the two photographs I was able to build this vital building. Much later I was to receive a 4 mm drawing and photographs from a fellow modeller, but I had already by then built the box - such is life.

Closer examination of one particular plan at a scale of 40 ft to 1 inch established a natural L-shaped layout, finishing at the Lower Trenneck bridge. This, in modelling terms, offered a pleasant scenic break before the fiddle yard. Consideration still had to be given to size and after much deliberation the carriage shed end of the layout was slightly compressed without loss of operating character. The final configuration is three boards of 3 ft by 22 in., and a curve section of 3 ft by 4 ft with a photographic display piece installed to make a flowing curve. This display does, I hope interest visitors at exhibitions. The complete layout is 12 ft long by 4 ft deep, plus the fiddle yard section, the latter representing Nancegollan and Gwinear Road.

Before moving into the modelling aspect I decided to build the model without the serpentine siding which connected with the loading dock. Evidence to hand had shown this particular siding was installed, then removed and later re-instated.

My attention now turned to the buildings which had to be accurate, with atmosphere. Drawings were already available for most buildings, albeit in 2 mm scale and I proceeded to re-scale to 3 mm using modern technology! A site visit is a must for anybody undertaking such a project and one such visit was made. Unfortunately all that remained was the goods shed, together with part of the station platform and the end of the loading dock. This type of visit gives a mental picture of the area and encourages you, particularly when you consider that my model was of a station which closed over 20 years before I started the project.

The goods shed is an example of information and site research all coming together, as at the Gwinear Road end of the shed there had been three different types of doors - sliding, opening and roller shutters, which had been fitted at various stages of its life.

Above: A photograph of the 3 mm = 1 ft scale model of Helston station constructed by Keith Gowen.
Keith Gowen

Right: A train from Gwinear Road, hauled bunker-first by a GWR prairie tank, approaches the road overbridge at the northern end of Helston station. Crossing the bridge is a GWR three-wheel 'mechanical horse' with a container loaded onto its flat bed trailer.
Keith Gowen

APPENDIX

Two views across the goods yard of Keith Gowen's model of Helston station. Note the cattle dock and yard crane. In the lower view the loading gauge can be seen standing over the exit to the goods yard and the engine shed is at the extreme right of the picture. *(Both) Keith Gowen*

The branch local has just arrived behind a '45XX' class 2-6-2T. *Keith Gowen*

Further views of the Helston branch model; the Gweek Coal Co. depot being particularly interesting. *Keith Gowen*

APPENDIX

The site visit confirmed this and I have chosen the 'opening door' period. Colour photographs were taken and I was fortunate to obtain colour prints of other buildings taken just after closure which gave me a record to find the correct colour balance. This blending and balancing of colour can take several hours, but the end result is worthwhile. These points give the building the right feel and atmosphere needed.

It became clear that I was missing a lot of information about three buildings behind the goods shed, these being a garage, store and coal shed. Although my GWR water supply plan gave the shape and floor dimensions, I had no photographic information. Regrettably we railway enthusiasts and modellers never take photographs of the right things as we are too interested in the engine or train!

I began to challenge my earlier objective in creating an accurate model and how I would overcome this problem when, by chance, three photographs came my way. It appeared that the coal shed and store were actually owned by Gweek & Co. Ltd, coal merchants in that area. The coal shed is an interesting model as I have chosen to build the model in a run-down state with coal 'oozing out'. It was sited on the point into the goods shed road, which is fine in reality but a major operational problem in model form when parking coal wagons. This little feature also gave one further headache - trying to find out the colour of the coal merchant's lorry. This was resolved by Derek Martin who contacted a retired driver, Mr Ernest Pascoe. The colour was a 'darkish green' and their vehicles were mostly Austins, although at one point a couple were ex-War Department. Not forgetting that I was building a model railway, the operational aspect had to be considered. At this point a visit to the National Railway Museum at York provided the working timetable details needed to develop a programme for exhibition running.

I have tried to supply the reader with assistance in how I modelled Helston, however, it must be remembered that as a prototype modeller I am re-creating history as portrayed at a specific time, day and year. It is with this mind that after 25 years exhibiting the model at well over 150 model railway exhibitions throughout the country, both at local and national level, it now resides as a permanent non-working model in the Helston Museum.

I believe the model is convincing simply because the exhibition visitor remembers it and now the residents of Helston, can talk about 'their railway' as they are reminded of the fact there once was a railway station in their town.

A GWR 'mechanical horse' delivery lorry stands at the north end of Helston station in this view of Keith Gowen's model. *Keith Gowen*

Bibliography and Further Reading

At first glance, the following list would appear to contain ample material on the West Cornwall Railway, but on closer examination it will be seen that many of the listed books and articles relate to locomotives, rather than railway history. There have, nevertheless, been a number of useful references to the Helston branch in books and articles, while a considerable amount of work has been undertaken at various times on mining and other aspects of Cornish local history. Some of the many books available on this interesting county have been included in the bibliography.

Anthony, G.H., *The Hayle, West Cornwall & Helston Railways*, Oakwood Press (1968)
Barton, D.B., *A History of Copper Mining in Cornwall* (1961)
Bennett, A., The Making of the Cornish Riviera, *Railway World*, April 1984
Clarke, R.H., *A Historical Survey of Great Western Stations* Vol. II, OPC (1979)
Clinker, C.R., *The Railways of Cornwall 1809-1963*, David & Charles (1963)
Cummings, John, *Railway Motor Buses & Bus Services* (1980)
Curnow, W.H., *Industrial Archaeology of Cornwall*
Dent, A.E.C., Early GWR Road Services, *Railway Magazine*, September 1952.
English, Pat, The Helston Branch, *Model Railway News*, January 1967
English, Pat, Praze Station, *Model Railway News*, March 1967
English, Pat, The Helston Branch, *Model Railway News*, January 1967
English, Pat, The Helston Branch, *Model Railway News*, January 1967
English, Pat, Gwinear Road Station, *Model Railway News*, February 1967
Fairclough, A. The *Story of Cornwall's Railways*, Tor Mark Press (1970)
Falmouth Packet, The passim
Freezer, Cyril J., Locomotives of the GWR: The Smallest Prairies, *Railway Modeller*, December 1968
Freezer, Cyril J., Locomotives of the GWR: The 45XXs, *Railway Modeller*, January 1969
Freezer, Cyril J., Locomotives of the GWR: No.34, *Railway Modeller*, March 1968
Great Western Railway, *Traffic Dealt with at Stations & Goods Depots, passim* (PRO RAIL 253/45)
Great Western Railway, *Holiday Haunts, passim*
Great Western Railway, *Towns, Villages, Outlying Works etc* (1938)
Great Western Railway, *Working & Public Timetables, passim*
Great Western Railway, Station Accounts Instruction Book (1929)
Great Western Railway, Register of Private Sidings
Great Western Railway, Census of Staff (1922, 1925 & 1929)
Great Western Railway, Signalling alteration, working notices etc, *passim*
Hamilton Jenkin, A.K., *Cornish Seafarers* (1932)
Hamilton Jenkin, A.K., *Cornwall & the Cornish* (1933)
Hamilton Jenkin, A.K., *Cornish Homes & Customs* (1934)
Hamilton Jenkin, A.K., *The Cornish Miner* (1927)
Harrison, Ian, *Great Western Railway Locomotive Allocations for 1921*, Wild Swan Publications (1984)
Heaps, Chris, The Helston Railway 1887-1964, *Railway World* November 1964
Helston Railway Company, minute books, etc.
Howsam, David, Porthleven, *Railway Modeller*, July 1967
Jenkins, Stanley C., *The Helston Branch Railway*, Oakwood Press (1992)
Jenkins, Stanley C., The Helston Branch, *Back Track*, November-December 1989
Jenkins, Stanley C., Steam Days at Penzance, *Steam Days* No. 152, April 2002
Jenkins, Stanley C. & Langley, Roger, *The West Cornwall Railway*, Oakwood Press (2002)
Journal of the House of Commons, passim
Journal of the House of Lords, passim

Kelly's Directories, passim
Lyons, Eric, *An Illustrated History of Great Western Locomotive Sheds*, OPC (1972)
MacDermot, E.T. *History of the Great Western Railway*, Vol. II, GWR (1927)
Matthews, Jack, The Helston Goods, *Great Western Railway Journal* No. 55 Summer 2005
Noall, Cyril, *A History of Cornish Mail & Stage Coaches*
Nock, O.S., *History of the Great Western Railway*, Vol. III, Ian Allan (1967)
Pryer, G.A., Signal Box Diagrams: Helston, *Railway Modeller*, January 1972
Proceedings of the Institute of Civil Engineers, passim
Railway Clearing House, *Handbook of Stations* (1910)
Railway Clearing House, *Handbook of Stations* (1938)
Railway Clearing House, *Handbook of Stations* (1922)
Railway Observer, The, passim
Railway Times, The, passim
Royal Cornwall Gazette, The, passim
Salmon, Arthur J., *The Little Guide to Cornwall* (1903)
Semmens, P.W.B., 'The Most Westerly & Southerly Branches', *Trains Illustrated*, June 1952
Semmens, P.W.B., *The Heyday of Great Western Train Services*, David & Charles (1990)
St John Thomas, David, *A Regional History of the Railways of Great Britain*:
   Vol. I *The West Country*, David & Charles (1960)
Track Layout Diagrams of the GWR: *Section 10 West Cornwall*, R.A. Cooke (1995)
Truscott, J.B., *The Church of England School Log Book, Helston*
West Briton, The, passim
Woodfin, R.J., *The Cornwall Railway* (1972)

Sources

Material for *The Helston Branch* was obtained from a variety of different sources. The pre-history of the line was put together with the aid of contemporary journals such as *Bradshaw's Shareholders' Manual*, and newspapers such as *The Times*, the *Railway Times* and the *West Briton*. Other useful sources for the early periods were the *House of Commons Journal*, the *House of Lords Journal* and the various Acts which eventually resulted at the end of the Parliamentary process.

Other primary sources for the Helston Railway from 1882 until 1898 included the Helston Railway Directors' minute book and the company's half-yearly reports. This information was supplemented by material culled from Board of Trade reports, *Bradshaw's Timetables*, and the *Proceedings of the Institute of Civil Engineers*.

Data relating to the later history of the branch was obtained from various GWR books, timetables and reports, local trade directories, contemporary newspapers, Ordnance Survey maps, and specialist journals such as the *Railway Magazine*, the *Railway Observer*, the *Railway World*, the *Great Western Railway Magazine*, and the *British Railways Magazine*.

Index

Accidents during construction, 30, 81
Aerodromes, 73, 81, 136, 137
Anglican Church and churches, 95
Ashburton branch, 103, 125
Armoured trains, 73,74
Bain, Daniel Wise, 18, 36
Bay of Panama, wrecked near Porthallow, 39
Beeching, Dr Richard, 147
Belfast & Northern Counties Railway, 51
Bickford-Smith, William, 14, 15, 18, 24, 25, 28, 33, 35, 36, 40, 41, 103, 151
Blenheim & Woodstock, 67,69
Bolitho, T.S., 14
Bolitho, William, 18, 22, 24, 28, 36
Bourton-on-the-Water, 69
Breage, 7, 59, 67, 68, 103
Broccoli and other vegetable traffic, 13, 65, 81, 95, 103 *et seq.*
Brunel, Isambard Kingdom, 10, 115
Buses, *see Road motor services*
Cadgwith, 36 *et seq.*, 51, 68
Camborne, 9, 14, 17
Camping coaches, 103, 107
Carbis Bay, 50
Cober viaduct, 7, 15, 22, 23, 26, 27, 30, 31, 33, 35, 108 *et seq.*, 151, 152
Cober, River and valley, 7, 8, 15, 22, 109
Coinagehall Street, 7, 8, 16, 20, 21
'Cornish Riviera Express', 49
Cornwall Motor Transport Co., 59
Cornwall Railway, 12 *et seq.*, 81
Cornwall Union Railway, 13
Coverack, 36, 37, 60, 68
Coverack Stone Co., 36
Crowan, 18, 87, 95
Culdrose aerodrome, 73, 81, 105, 136, 137, 156
Dieselization, 145
Daniell, J.R., 14, 15
East Lovel mine, 36
Explosion at Helston, 57, 59
Falmouth branch, 12 *et seq.*, 17, 36, 37, 49, 81, 144, 155, 156
Faringdon branch, 67, 69
Flora Day, 51, 66, 136
Fulton, Robert (1765-1815), 8
Ganger's occupation key system, 70
Gooch, Sir Daniel (1816-89), 29, 30
Gravatt, William, 115
Great Blizzard of 1891, The, 37, 38, 127
Grierson, James (1827-87), 25
Grylls, S. Morley, 13
Gunwalloe, 59, 68
Gweek, 8, 11, 13, 68
Gwennap mines, 9
Gwinear Road 14, 15, 17, 18, 22, 23, 25 *et seq.*, 30, 33, 35, 37, 39, 42, 48 *et seq.*, 73 *et seq.*, 87, 141, 150, 159 *et passim*

Hayle, 9, 10, 17
Hayle Railway, 9, 10, 11, 74
Helford River, 8
Helston, 7 *et seq.*, 13, 26 *et seq.*, 35, 43, 49, 53, 56, 57, 62, 109 *et seq.*, 147, 151,159 *et passim*
Helston & Penryn Junction Railway, 13, 14, 41
Helston Canal, proposed, 8
Helston Museum, 5, 21, 151
Helston Railway,
  Closure of, 147 *et seq.*
  Construction of, 19 *et seq.*
  Early years of, 36 *et seq.*
  Formation of, 14 *et seq.*
  Opening of, 32 *et seq.*
Helston Railway Preservation Co., 155, 156
Helston Union Workhouse, 8, 19, 22, 28, 29
Helston gas works, 66
James, William, 9
Jenkin, Alfred, 13
Jenkin, Sylvanus W. (1821-1911), 14, 22 *et seq.*, 28, 32, 36, 115
Kendall, John, 13
Lang, Thomas, 25 *et seq.*, 30, 41
Lanhydrock House, 13, 41
Lizard, The 14 *et seq.*, 28, 37, 41, 44, 49, 51, 52, 54, 57, 68, 73, 111, 119, 145
Liskeard & Caradon Railway, 36
Lizard Light Railway, proposed, 41, 44, 51
Lowerton, 23, 30, 33, 68, 151
Lynton & Barnstaple Railway, 51, 59
Maddison, Edward Charles, 19, 24, 30
Margary, Peter John (1820-96), 27, 115
Martyn, Richard Skewes, 18, 21, 24
Model railway of Helston, 161 *et seq.*
Moretonhampstead branch, 125
Motive power, 6, 49, 50, 65, 125, 137 *et seq.*, 157
Mullion, 37, 38, 59, 67, 68, 73
Murdock, William, 9
Nancegollan, 8, 22, 28, 32, 33, 35, 37, 73, 94 *et seq.*, 142, 143, 147, 150, 159
Nationalization, effects of, 137, 145
Navvies, railway, 21, 22, 24, 25, 30, 31, 33
Newcomen, Thomas (1663-1729), 9
Newquay branch, 93
Olver, Thomas & Sons, 81
Overend, Gurney & Co., 14
Oxfordshire & Buckinghamshire Light Infantry, 73
Penryn, 9, 11, 13 *et seq.*, 17, 81, 155
Penryn & Helston Railways & Tramways, 14
Penzance, 10 *et seq.*, 17, 25, 50, 63
Poldice Tramroad, 9
Porthallow, 37, 59, 67, 68

Porthlevan, 15, 57, 59, 67, 68, 101
Porthoustock, 37, 59, 67, 68
Portreath, 9,10
Praze, 22, 28, 33, 35, 37, 42, 70, 86 *et seq.*, 147, 150, 159
Predanack aerodrome, 73
Quarry traffic, 13, 36, 65, 69, 111, 114, 115
Railway Mania, The, 11
Redruth, 9, 10, 13, 17, 36, 63
Redruth & Chacewater Railway, 9
Reformation, The, 7
Rich, Colonel Francis, 31
Road motor services, 51 *et seq.*, 63, 67, 145, 148
Robartes, Thomas Agar, 13, 41
Rogers, John Jope, 13
Rolling stock, 37,65, 66, 137
Rous, Richard G., 18, 24, 36
Ruan Minor, 57, 58, 68
Rural delivery services, 67 *et seq.*, 129
Signalling, 6, 27, 39, 45, 70, 81, 93 *et seq.*, 100, 101, 111, 113, 121, 128, 129
Shipston-on-Stour branch, 35
St Aubyn, John, 13, 41
St Aubyn, W. Molesworth, 14, 24 *et seq.*, 28, 36, 41
St Ives branch, 11, 37, 49, 50, 115, 127, 144
St Keverne, 57, 59, 68
Staines West branch, 152
Tickets and fare, 144, 145, 153, 155
Tin mining industry, 7, 8, 13, 14, 36, 41, 95
Tourists and holiday traffic, 15, 37, 49, 50, 51, 71
Traffic statistics, 87, 93, 101, 107, 127, 136
Train services and timetables, 37, 39, 40, 45 *et seq.*, 55, 63 *et seq.*, 73, 74
Tregadjack Farm, proposed station, 22, 35
Tresavean mine, 9
Tetbury branch, 35, 152
Trevarno, 5, 28, 103, 155
Trevithick, Richard (1771-1833), 9
Truro, 10 *et seq.*, 17, 144
Truthall Halt, 35, 106 *et seq.*, 147, 152, 156, 159
Vyvyan, Reverend Sir Vyell, 36
Wendron, 7, 9, 13, 14, 18, 22, 35, 68
West Cornwall Railway, 10 *et seq.*, 14, 15, 18, 37, 75, 77, 109, 127
Western National Omnibus Co., 63, 113, 115, 119, 150
Wheal Buller, 9
Wheal Crofty, 9
Wheal Vor, 7, 13, 31
Wheal Vor axe murder, 31
World War I, 50, 57, 59, 61, 67, 73, 93, 123, 127, 153
World War II, 51, 70 *et seq.*, 101, 137, 151